Guardians of the Land:
Indigenous Peoples and the Health of the Earth

Alan Thein Durning

Vikram Krishna Akula, Research Assistant

Ed Ayres, Editor

Worldwatch Paper 112
December 1992

Sections of this paper may be reproduced in magazines and newspapers with acknowledgment to the Worldwatch Institute. The views expressed are those of the author and do not necessarily represent those of the Worldwatch Institute and its directors, officers, or staff, or of funding organizations.

Printed on 100% recycled paper containing 15% post-consumer waste

Table of Contents

Introduction

In July 1992, Tulalang Maway—an aged tribal chief with a price on his head—sat at the base of the Philippines' tallest volcano and made a simple plea. "Our Christian brothers are enjoying their life here in the plains," said the 86-year-old Lumad leader, sweeping his arm toward the agricultural fields his tribe long ago ceded to immigrants. Turning toward Mount Apo—a Lumad sacred site that he has vowed to defend against energy development "to the last drop of blood"—Maway slowly finished his thought, "We only ask them to leave us our last sanctuary."[1]

Chief Maway's entreaty could have been voiced by almost any tribal Filipino, or, for that matter, any Native American, Australian aborigine, or member of one of the world's nearly five thousand other distinct indigenous cultures. All have ancient ties to the land, water, and wildlife of their ancestral domains, and all are endangered by onrushing forces of the outside world. They have been decimated by plagues and violence. Their cultures have been altered by missionaries and exploited by entrepreneurs. Their subsistence economies have been dismantled by the agents of national development. And their homelands have been overrun by commercial resource extractors and landless peasants.

In fact, Maway's plea was all too familiar: native peoples want their lands to be spared further abuse, they want their birthright returned to them. It is an appeal so old that it seems almost a relic of the past—evoking the tone long ago struck by Black Elk, holy man of the Oglala Sioux: "Once we were happy in our own country and we were seldom hungry, for then the two-leggeds and the four-leggeds lived together like relatives, and there was plenty for them and for us. But the wasichus

I would like to acknowledge Julian Burger, Don Dumond, Gail Fondahl, Gus Gatmaytan, Bob Hitchcock, Barbara Johnston, Owen Lynch, and Ted Macdonald for their comments on an early draft of this paper. I am grateful to the Legal Rights and Natural Resources Center of Quezon City, Philippines, for arranging and accompanying me on research visits to tribal Filipino communities in July 1992. My heartfelt thanks to the indigenous peoples of the Philippines who so generously shared their experiences, their struggles, and their homes with me.

[whites] came, and they have made little islands for us and other little islands for the four-leggeds, and always these islands are becoming **6** smaller, for around surges the gnawing flood of the wasichus."[2]

For people living in the world's modern nation-states, it may be easy to associate present cases with this tragic but unredeemable past, and—perhaps with fleeting pangs of guilt—to regretfully discount indigenous claims as hopeless. The contest between industrial societies and native peoples is so lopsided that supporting indigenous cultures may seem quixotic. The ethical and humanitarian justification for such support—the sanctity of human rights, the intrinsic value of each culture, the devastating alienation suffered when a people's culture is severed from them—has always been there, but the political motivation has not.

There may also be a tendency to believe that even if the task of protecting these endangered cultures were not quixotic, it would be too little, too late—a case of closing the barn door after the barn has burned. Indigenous peoples get little attention in the mainstream media, and what little they get often implies that people like Chief Maway are the few remaining holdouts of a way of life that is, in any case, now largely gone.

But both of these perceptions are mistaken. Far from disappearing, the world's indigenous people number in the hundreds of millions; and far from hopeless, their cause is gaining ground where it never did before. Today, five centuries after Christopher Columbus sailed to the Americas and opened the European expansion that has spelled the end for so many native peoples, there are two compelling reasons for the world's dominant societies to heed the voices of indigenous peoples more seriously than they ever have. These reasons bear not only on the lives—and ways of life—of the threatened peoples, but on those of the dominant ones as well.

First, indigenous peoples are the sole guardians of vast, little-disturbed habitats that modern societies depend on more than they may realize—to regulate water cycles, maintain the stability of the climate, and provide valuable plants, animals, and genes. Their homelands may harbor more endangered plant and animal species than all the world's nature reserves. Second, they possess, in their ecological knowledge, an asset of incalculable value: a map to the biological diversity of the earth on which all life depends. Encoded in indigenous languages, customs, and practices may be as much understanding of nature as is stored in the libraries of modern science.

It was little appreciated in past centuries of exploitation, but is undeniable now, that the world's dominant cultures cannot sustain the earth's ecological health without the aid of the world's endangered cultures. Biological diversity—of paramount importance both to sustaining viable ecosystems and to improving human existence through scientific advances—is inextricably linked to cultural diversity.

Hopes for more effective support of indigenous peoples are now being raised not only by the recognition that their protection is valuable to all humankind, but by their growing ability to help fend off traditional forms of exploitation. Over the past few decades, hundreds of native groups have organized politically—and joined forces—to defend their resources and ways of life, and can therefore put aid from friendly quarters to better use than ever before.

If indigenous peoples have a large, perhaps pivotal, role to play in sustaining the earth as guardians of critical habitats and biological riches, they may have an equally important role as cultural models for the world's more populous societies. "Over the past few generations," writes Jeffrey A. McNeely, chief ecologist of the Geneva-based World Conservation Union, "a fundamental ecological shift has occurred. The world's collection of highly diverse adaptations to local environmental conditions has been replaced by a world culture dominated by very high levels of material consumption." If that world culture is to survive and prosper it will have to learn much about conservation, environmental ethics, and regard for future generations. Where better to learn than from the indigenous cultures that have been manifesting such values for centuries?[3]

From the Philippines to upstate New York, indigenous peoples are fighting for their ancestral territories. They are struggling in courts and

8 national parliaments, gaining power through new mass movements and international campaigns, and—as on the slopes of Mount Apo—defending their inheritance with their lives. They have resoundingly answered any questions about the importance or viability of their cause, and only one question remains: Who will stand with them?

State of the Nations

Indigenous peoples (or "native" or "tribal" peoples) populate parts of every continent and most countries. (See Table 1.) They include groups as disparate as the Quechua of Bolivia, Ecuador, and Peru—descendants of the Incan civilization—who collectively number more than 10 million, and the Gurumalum band of Papua New Guinea who number fewer than ten. The extreme variations in their ways of life and current circumstances defy ready definition. Indeed, states manipulate definitions to suit their political needs, variously labeling indigenous peoples "small nationalities," "remote area dwellers," "mountain peasants," "backward tribes," "primitive populations," and so on. Many anthropologists, in contrast, insist that indigenous peoples be defined only as they define themselves: each group thinks of itself as a distinct people.[4]

Still, within the inexhaustible diversity of their ways of life, many indigenous cultures share a number of characteristics that help describe, if not define, them. They are typically descendants of the original inhabitants of an area taken over by more powerful outsiders. They are distinct from their country's dominant group in language, culture, or religion. Most think of themselves as custodians and caretakers—not owners—of their land and other resources, and partly define themselves by reference to the habitat from which they draw their livelihood. They commonly live in or maintain strong ties to a subsistence economy; many are, or are descendants of, hunter-gatherers, fishers, nomadic or seasonal herders, shifting forest farmers, or subsistence peasant cultivators. And their social relations are often tribal, involving collective management of natural resources, thick networks of bonds among individuals, and group decision making, often by consensus among elders.[5]

Measured by spoken languages—the single best indicator of distinct cultures because each language implicitly encapsulates a unique view of the universe—all the world's people belong to 6,000 cultures; 4,000 to 5,000 of these are indigenous ones. Of the 5.5 billion humans on the planet, roughly 200 to 600 million are indigenous people. (These ranges are wide because of varying definitions of "indigenous"; the higher figures include ethnic nations that lack political autonomy, such as Tibetans, Kurds, and Zulus, while the lower figures count only smaller, subnational societies.) In some countries, especially those settled by Europeans in the past five centuries, indigenous populations are fairly easy to count. (See Table 2.) By contrast, lines between indigenous peoples and ethnic minorities are difficult to draw in Asia and Africa, where cultural diversity remains greatest.[6]

9

Regardless of where lines are drawn, however, human cultures are disappearing at unprecedented rates. Worldwide, the loss of cultural diversity is keeping pace with the loss of biological diversity. Anthropologist Jason Clay of Cultural Survival in Cambridge, Massachusetts, writes, "there have been more...extinctions of tribal peoples in this century than in any other in history." Brazil alone lost 87 tribes in the first half of the century. One third of North American languages and two-thirds of Australian languages have disappeared since 1800—the overwhelming share of them since 1900.[7]

Cultures are dying out even faster than the peoples who belong to them. University of Alaska linguist Michael Krauss projects that half the world's languages—the storehouses of peoples' intellectual heritages and the scaffolding for their unique understandings of life—will disappear within a century. These 3,000 languages, and arguably the cultures they embody, are no longer passed on to sufficient numbers of children to ensure their survival. Krauss likens such cultures to animal species doomed to extinction because their populations are below the threshold needed for adequate reproduction. Only 5 percent of all languages, moreover, enjoy the relative safety of having at least a half-million speakers.[8]

To trace the history of indigenous peoples' subjugation is simply to recast the story of the rise of the world's dominant cultures: the spread of

Table 1. Indigenous Peoples of the World, 1992

Region	Characteristics of Peoples[1]
Africa and Middle East	Great cultural diversity found throughout the continent; "indigenous" share hotly contested. Some 25-30 million nomadic herders in East Africa, Sahel, and Arabian peninsula include Bedouin, Dinka, Masai, and Turkana. San (Bushmen) of Namibia and Botswana and pygmies of central African rain forest, both traditionally hunter-gatherers, have occupied present homelands for at least 20,000 years. *25-350 million people; 2,000 languages spoken.*
Americas	Native Americans concentrated near centers of ancient civilizations: Aztec in Mexico, Mayan in Central America, and Incan in Andes. In Latin America, most farm small plots; in North America, 2 million Indians live in cities and reservations. *42 million people; 900 languages spoken.*
Arctic	Inuit (Eskimo) and other Arctic peoples of North America, Greenland, and Siberia traditionally fishers, whalers, and hunters. Sami (Lapp) of Arctic Scandinavia traditionally reindeer herders. *2 million people; 50 languages spoken.*
East Asia	Chinese indigenous peoples, numbering up to 82 million, mostly subsistence farmers such as Bulang of south China or former pastoralists such as ethnic Mongolians of north and west China. Ainu of Japan and aboriginal Taiwanese now largely industrial laborers. *12-84 million people; 150 languages spoken.*

Table 1. (continued)

Region	Characteristics of Peoples	11

Oceania

Aborigines of Australia and Maoris of New Zealand, traditionally farmers, fishers, hunters, and gatherers. Many now raise livestock. Islanders of South Pacific continue to fish and harvest marine resources. *3 million people; 500 languages spoken.*

South Asia

Gond, Bhil, and other adivasis, or tribal peoples, inhabit forest belt of central India. Adivasis of Bangladesh concentrated in Chittagong hills on Burmese border; several million tribal farmers and pastoralists in Afghanistan, Pakistan, Nepal, Iran, and Central Asian republics of former U.S.S.R. *74-91 million people; 700 languages spoken.*

Southeast Asia

Tribal Hmong, Karen, and other forest-farming peoples form ethnic mosaic covering uplands. Indigenous population proportional to distribution of forest: Laos has most forest and tribal peoples, Myanmar and Vietnam have less of each, and Thailand and mainland Malaysia have least. Tribal peoples concentrated at ends of Philippine and Indonesian archipelagos. Island of New Guinea mostly indigenous tribes. *32-55 million people; 1,950 languages spoken.*

---

[1]Estimated indigenous populations vary widely based on definition of "indigenous." All languages (not just indigenous) are counted, to give overall indicator of cultural diversity.

Source: Worldwatch Institute, based on sources in endnote 4.

Table 2. Estimated Populations of Indigenous Peoples, Selected Countries, 1992

Country	Indigenous Population[1]	Share of National Population
	(million)	(percent)
Papua New Guinea	3.0	77
Bolivia	5.6	70
Guatemala	4.6	47
Peru	9.0	40
Ecuador	3.8	38
Myanmar	14.0	33
Laos	1.3	30
Mexico	10.9	12
New Zealand	0.4	12
Chile	1.2	9
Philippines	6.0	9
India	63.0	7
Malaysia	0.8	4
Canada	0.9	4
Australia	0.4	2
Brazil	1.5	1
Bangladesh	1.2	1
Thailand	0.5	1
United States	2.0	1
former Soviet Union	1.4	<1

[1]Generally excludes those of mixed ancestry.

Source: Worldwatch Institute, based on sources in endnote 6.

Han Chinese into Central and Southeast Asia, the ascent of Aryan empires on the Indian subcontinent, the southward advance of Bantu cultures across Africa, and the creation of a world economy first through European colonialism and then through industrial development. Surviving indigenous cultures are often but tattered remnants of their predecessors' societies.[9]

When Columbus reached the New World in 1492, there were perhaps 54 million people in the Americas, almost as many as in Europe at the time. Their numbers plummeted, however, as plagues radiated from the landfalls of the conquistadors. Five centuries later, the indigenous peoples of the Americas, numbering some 42 million, have yet to match their earlier population. Similar contractions followed the arrival of Europeans in Australia, New Zealand, and Siberia.[10]

Worldwide, virtually no indigenous peoples remain entirely isolated from national societies. By indoctrination or brute force, nations have assimilated native groups into their cultural mainstreams. As a consequence, few follow the ways of their ancestors unchanged. Just one-tenth of the Penan hunter-gatherers, for example, continue to hunt in the rain forests of Malaysian Borneo. A similar fraction of the Sami (Lapp) reindeer herders of northern Scandinavia accompany their herds on the Arctic ranges. Half of North American Indians dwell in cities, as do many New Zealand Maori.[11]

Indigenous peoples whose cultures are besieged frequently end up on the bottom of the national economy. They are often the first sent to war for the state, as in Namibia and the Philippines, and the last to go to work: unemployment in Canadian Indian communities averages 50 percent. They are overrepresented among migrant laborers in India, beggars in Mexico, and uranium miners in the United States. They are often drawn into the shadow economy: they grow drug crops in northern Thailand, run gambling casinos in the United States, and sell their daughters into prostitution in Taiwan. Everywhere, racism against them is rampant. India's adivasis, or tribal people, endure hardships comparable to those of the "untouchables," the most downtrodden caste.[12]

Whatever the indicator of human welfare, native peoples rank at the bottom among races. Aboriginal Australians' lives are 18 years shorter than those of non-aboriginal Australians. Guatemalan Indians' per capita income is a tenth of the national average. India's tribal peoples have a literacy rate one-third that of people in India overall. Siberian indigenous peoples' rates of infant mortality and tuberculosis infection are twice the Russian norm.[13]

Native peoples' inferior social status is sometimes codified in national law and perpetuated by institutionalized abuse. Many members of the hill tribes in Thailand are denied citizenship, as are tribal people in Cambodia, and until 1988 the Brazilian constitution legally classified Indians as minors and wards of the state.[14]

In the extreme, nation-states are simply genocidal: Burmese soldiers systemically raped, murdered, and enslaved thousands of Arakanese villagers in early 1992. Guatemala has exterminated perhaps 100,000 Mayans in its three-decade counterinsurgency; forensic anthropologists have recently begun exhuming mass graves containing hundreds of mutilated bodies in the nation's high country. Perhaps another 200,000 have died in East Timor and Irian Jaya since 1970, at the hands of Indonesian forces intent on solidifying their power. Of the 105 armed conflicts occurring in different parts of the world in 1992, 74 pitted a state against a people that lived within its borders, according to geographer Bernard Nietschmann of the University of California, Berkeley.[15]

In much of the world, the oppression that indigenous peoples suffer has indelibly marked their own psyches, manifesting itself in depression and social disintegration. Says Tamara Gliminova of the Khant people of Siberia, "When they spit into your soul for this long, there is little left."[16]

Homelands

Indigenous peoples not yet engulfed in modern societies live mostly by what Mexican anthropologist Gonzalo Aguirre Beltran called "regions of refuge"— places so rugged, inaccessible, or remote that they have been little disturbed by the industrial economy. They remain in these areas for tragic reasons. In most cases, peoples in more fertile lands were either eradicated outright to make way for settlers and plantations, or forced to retreat—sometimes at gun point—into these natural redoubts. Whereas indigenous peoples exercised de facto control over most of the earth's ecosystems as recently as two centuries ago, the territory they now occupy is reduced to an estimated 12 to 19 percent of the earth's land area—depending, again, on where the line between indigenous peoples and ethnic nations is drawn. And even on that diminishing fragment, little of the land is recognized as theirs by the national governments.[17]

For most indigenous peoples, gaining legal protection for the remainder of their subsistence base has the highest political priority. If they lose this struggle, their cultures stand little chance of surviving. As the World Council of Indigenous Peoples, a global federation based in Canada, wrote in 1985, "Next to shooting indigenous peoples, the surest way to kill us is to separate us from our part of the Earth." Most native peoples are bound to their land through relationships that are practical, spiritual, and historical. They have come to know the land through the timeless repetition of daily routine, have imbued it with meaning through the long elaboration of myths and legends, and have defended it in the defining events of their cultural past. Tribal Filipino Edtami Mansayagan, attempting to communicate the anguish of witnessing the destruction of the rivers, valleys, meadows, and hillsides of his people's mountain domain, exclaims, "these are the living pages of our unwritten history." The question of who shall control resources in the regions of refuge is the crux of indigenous survival.[18]

Intact indigenous communities and little-disturbed ecosystems overlap with singular regularity, from the coastal swamps of South America to the shifting sands of the Sahara, from the ice floes of the circumpolar north to the coral reefs of the South Pacific. For example, when a National Geographic Society team in Washington, D.C., compiled a map of Indian lands and remaining forest cover in Central America in 1992, they confirmed the personal observation of Geodisio Castillo, a Kuna Indian from Panama. "Where there are forests there are indigenous people," he said, "and where there are indigenous people there are forests." Likewise, in the Philippines and Thailand, little more than a third of the land officially zoned as forest remains forest-covered; the tracts that do still stand are largely those tended by tribal people. Even in the last decade of the twentieth century, many of the world's little-disturbed habitats owe their survival to native stewards.[19]

If indigenous homelands make up a substantial share of the globe's unscathed ecosystems, they harbor an even larger share of its biological diversity, for two reasons. First, because populations of both indigenous peoples and unique plant and animal species are numerically concentrated in remnant habitats in the tropics, the biosphere's most species-rich habitats are usually homes to endangered cultures. This relationship between cultural diversity and biological diversity stands out even in global statistics. Just nine countries together account for 60 percent of human languages. Of these nine centers of cultural diversity, six are also on the roster of what biologists call "megadiversity" countries—those with exceptional numbers of unique plant and animal species. (See Figure 1.) Similarly, eight of the twelve megadiversity countries also rank at the top in cultural diversity, with more than 100 languages spoken in each.[20]

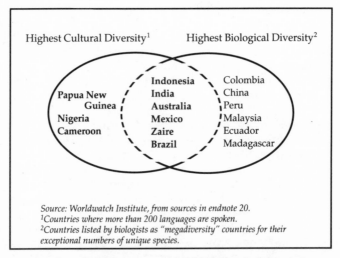

Highest Cultural Diversity[1]   Highest Biological Diversity[2]

Papua New Guinea
Nigeria
Cameroon

Indonesia
India
Australia
Mexico
Zaire
Brazil

Colombia
China
Peru
Malaysia
Ecuador
Madagascar

Source: Worldwatch Institute, from sources in endnote 20.
[1]Countries where more than 200 languages are spoken.
[2]Countries listed by biologists as "megadiversity" countries for their exceptional numbers of unique species.

**Figure 1: Cultural Diversity and Biological Diversity
Circa 1990**

Second, indigenous peoples have consciously increased the biological diversity they inherited from nature—not by creating new species, but by fostering genetic diversity within species—an achievement for which the world's ascendant cultures are deeply indebted to them. Modern societies depend on an ever narrowing range of genetic strains for their food and other products of the earth. Reserves of genetic diversity are crucial insurance in a global economy that has converted so many ecosystems to high-yielding but vulnerable monocultures. Crop fields, orchards, animal farms, tree plantations, pastures, fish runs—all have been turned into genetically-uniform super producers. In just 15 years, Indonesia has lost 1,500 varieties of rice, with just a few remaining varieties now dominating the country's production. The banks of genetic diversity that have repeatedly rescued such monocultures from pests, diseases, and changing soil and climate conditions are the fields, forests, and streams of indigenous peoples.[21]

Peoples such as the Kpelle of Liberia foster diversity for the security it produces; they carefully match crop strains with the slope, soil conditions, and sun light conditions on each patch of their land. Women of the forest-dwelling Kpelle sow more than 100 varieties of rice, making their fields jigsaw puzzles of genetic diversity. Such practices are so commonplace among indigenous cultivators that the International Society for Ethnobiology stated in 1988, "native peoples have been stewards of 99 percent of the world's genetic resources."[22]

While diverse indigenous cultures are primary caretakers of the earth's diverse biological resources, they are not hands-off conservationists interested in preserving nature in its pure, wild state. They are, and always have been, interested in using nature for their benefit; indeed, the history of that use throws into question the very idea of wild nature. Mexican ecologist Arturo Gómez Pompa writes, "virtually every part of the globe, from the boreal forests to the humid tropics, has been inhabited, modified, or managed throughout our human past." Of the earth's land area, only the ice-locked tenth in Antarctica and Greenland went largely untouched by humans before the industrial era.[23]

In the tropical forests of Southeast Asia and the Americas, for example, vast tracts were tended and transformed by tribal peoples over millenia.

Aboriginal Australians, like the plains dwellers of Africa and the Americas, used fire to convert forest to grassland, stimulate new grass growth, and increase animal populations. Animal and plant populations in most of the world reflect not just the blind logic of natural selection; they also reflect human selection.[24]

The essential difference between indigenous and industrial societies' uses of nature is scale. Indigenous peoples have changed habitats modestly. They have usually maintained the overall productivity of their homelands, sometimes as a fortuitous byproduct of their own small populations and low-impact technologies, and sometimes intentionally, through intricate local conservation regimes. Industrial societies, by contrast, too frequently exhaust habitats through overuse, degrade them beyond recovery, or simply strip them from the earth to make space for tree farms, factories, and shopping malls.

The economies of industrial societies continue to undermine native resources. Part of the problem is that, because of their direct dependence on the earth, indigenous peoples suffer more acutely from the deteriorating environmental conditions experienced by all peoples. The fallout from the 1986 nuclear accident at Chernobyl contaminated huge stretches of Sami grazing lands in northern Scandinavia, turning the Sami reindeer into walking radioactive waste sites. And mines, paper mills, and other industrial facilities have contaminated traditional fisheries all around the Pacific Rim. The problem is easily exacerbated by native peoples' political powerlessness. Virtually all of the nuclear weapon tests ever conducted, for example, have been on the ancestral lands of indigenous peoples too weak to fend off the military establishments of nuclear states: the Western Shoshone of Nevada, the Kiribati islanders of the Pacific, the Yakut and Komi peoples of Siberia, the Pitjantjatjara and other aboriginal peoples of Australia, the Uyghurs of western China, the Bedouins of southern Algeria, and many others.[25]

More significantly, however, it is because of their very success in conserving resources that indigenous peoples find these resources being exploited by industrial economies. Other peoples' natural wealth has been exhausted, so the world turns to native lands. Writes World Bank anthropologist Shelton Davis: " The creation of a...global economy...has

> "Virtually all the nuclear weapon tests ever conducted have been on the ancestral lands of indigenous peoples too weak to fend off the military establishments of nuclear states."

meant the pillage of native peoples' lands, labor and resources and their enforced acculturation and spiritual conquest. Each cycle of global economic expansion—the search for gold and spices in the sixteenth century, the fur trade and sugar estate economics of the seventeenth and eighteenth centuries, the rise of the great coffee, copra and...tropical fruit plantations in the late nineteenth and early twentieth centuries, the modern search for petroleum, strategic minerals, and tropical hardwoods—was based upon the exploitation of natural resources or primary commodities and led to the displacement of indigenous peoples and the undermining of traditional cultures."[26]

The juggernaut of the money economy has not slowed in the late twentieth century; if anything, it has accelerated. Soaring consumer demand among the world's fortunate, and burgeoning populations among the unfortunate, fuel the global economy's drive into native peoples' territories. Loggers, miners, commercial fishers, small farmers, plantation growers, dam builders, oil drillers—all come to seek their fortunes. Governments that equate progress with export earnings aid them, and military establishments bent on controlling far-flung territories often back them.[27]

Logging, in particular, is a menace because so many indigenous peoples dwell in woodlands. Japanese builders, for example, are devouring the ancient hardwood forests of tropical Borneo, home of the Penan and other Dayak peoples, for disposable concrete molds. Most mahogany exported from Latin America is now logged illegally on Indian reserves, and most non-plantation teak cut in Asia currently comes from tribal lands in the war-torn hills of Myanmar. As ethnomusicologist Marina Roseman of the University of Pennsylvania recently noted, "Their dream worlds are becoming our dream houses."[28]

Mining, too, has had ruinous consequences for native lands. In the late eighties, for instance, tens of thousands of gold prospectors infiltrated the remote northern Brazilian haven of the Yanomami, the last large, isolated group of indigenous peoples in the Americas. The miners turned streams into sewers, laced the food chain with the toxic mercury they used to purify gold, and precipitated an epidemic of malaria that killed more than a thousand children and elders. Just in time, the Brazilian government recognized and began defending the Yanomami homeland in early 1992, a rare and hopeful precedent in the annals of indigenous history. Still, in Brazil overall, mining concessions overlap 34 percent of Indian lands.[29]

Oil extraction has produced similarly destructive results. The swamp-land range of the reindeer-herding Khant and Mansi peoples of Siberia contains the richest oil deposits in Russia, but the reckless exploitation of those reserves is killing both the wetlands—the largest in the world—and the herders' way of life. Oil derricks there leak as much as one barrel of oil for each barrel they produce, spreading slicks over thousands of square kilometers of swamp grasses. Reindeer, wildlife, fish, and indigenous peoples suffer the consequences. Energy projects and other development pressures have rendered three-fourths of the Khant-Mansi lands—and the neighboring Nentsy lands—useless for hunting, fishing, and herding. Petroleum production has had similar consequences on scores of other peoples. Laments one Ecuadoran elder, whose people the Cofanes have been decimated since the sixties by Texaco operations in their rain forest domain, "Before, lots of wild boar. Before, lots of hunting. Before, no petroleum."[30]

Other energy projects, especially large dams, also take their toll on native habitats. In the north of Canada, the provincial electric utility Hydro Quebec in 1985 completed a massive project called James Bay I, inundating vast areas of Cree Indian hunting grounds and unexpectedly contaminating fisheries with naturally occurring heavy metals that previously had been bound up in the soil. The Cree and neighboring Inuit tribes have organized against the project's gigantic next phase, James Bay II. The $60-billion project would tame 11 wild rivers, altering an area the size of France to generate 27,000 megawatts of exportable power. Yet Matthew Coon-Come, Grand Chief of the Cree, says, "The only people who have the right to build dams on our territory are the beavers." Equally gargantuan schemes threaten millions of indigenous people in India and China.[31]

On the seas, the familiar pattern is repeated. Mechanized trawlers and factory fishing fleets have pushed into the coastal ranges of the world's 12 million small-boat fishers, many of whom are indigenous peoples.

The modern boats overtax near-shore fisheries and undermine local fishing traditions, which still provide one-third of all fish caught worldwide each year. Fleets from Taiwan, for example, regularly work the reefs of the Torres Strait between Australia and Papua New Guinea, in violation of both countries' laws and the fishing rights of the aboriginal islanders.[32]

Commercial producers have also taken over indigenous lands for large-scale agriculture. The Barabaig herders of Tanzania have lost more than 400 square kilometers of dry-season range to a mechanized wheat farm. Private ranchers in Botswana have enclosed grazing lands for their own use, and Australian ranchers have usurped aboriginal territory. In peninsular Malaysia, palm and rubber plantations have left the Orang Asli (Original People) with tiny fractions of their ancient tropical forests.[33]

Less dramatic but more pervasive is the ubiquitous invasion of small farmers. Sometimes sponsored by the state, but ultimately driven by population growth and maldistribution of farmland, poor settlers encroach on native lands everywhere. In Indonesia during the eighties, for example, the government shifted 2 million people from densely populated islands such as Java to 8,000 square kilometers of newly cleared plots in sparsely populated indigenous provinces such as Irian Jaya, Kalimantan, and Sumatra. Half the area settled was virgin forest—much of it indigenous territory.[34]

The appropriation of indigenous home ranges has been accomplished in part by appeal to specious legal doctrines, such as the now-discredited principle that *terra nullius* (empty or ungoverned territory) is free for the taking. Declaring most of the world beyond Europe "empty," colonial governments—and the independent states that followed them—staked claims to all lands that were not physically occupied or under permanent cultivation. With the stroke of a pen, states reserved for themselves forests, wetlands, drylands, mountain slopes, bodies of water, wildlife, fisheries, and the minerals in the earth. Ever since, states have dispensed these resources to private firms and others as suited their political ends.[35]

For native peoples, the result was summary dispossession. "In law," says attorney Gus Gatmaytan of the Manila-based Legal Rights and

Natural Resources Center, "the indigenous peoples of the Philippines are squatters in their own lands," because the Philippine state claims ownership of 62 percent of the country's territory. The story is the same around the world. Indonesia asserts its dominion over 74 percent of the nation's land, along with all waters and offshore fishing rights. The Thai Royal Forestry Department claims 40 percent of Thailand. The forest agencies of the states of India control, under law, 25 percent of national territory. Cameroon and Tanzania claim *all* forestland, as do most African states. Even Australia, which has returned large areas to aboriginal peoples since 1970, has kept all mineral rights in the hands of the state.[36]

States often have justified the nationalization of forests, fisheries, and other natural resources by invoking the specter of the "tragedy of the commons"—a pervasive but flawed theory of natural resource use which holds that shared resources are inevitably degraded because self-interest drives individuals to maximize short term gains or risk losing out to other resource users. Under this theory, only a central authority such as the state can enforce rules that prevent shared resources from becoming free-for-alls.[37]

The real tragedy of the commons, however, is that this authoritarian approach to resource management created the conditions it purported to avert. Many of the shared resources states arrogated to themselves had been effectively managed by indigenous peoples for centuries. Nationalizing them undercut the authority of local people's stewardship; indeed, it sometimes made enforcing customary regulations a criminal act. Tribal chiefs, for example, who, in accordance with traditional procedures, confiscated livestock from violators of grazing restrictions might be convicted of theft in state courts. When China weakened customary hunting restraints on the vast grasslands of Tibet, it created an unconstrained hunting frenzy that has obliterated wildlife herds.[38]

Nationalizing indigenous homelands, meanwhile, has left no alternative way of preventing resource grabbing. Almost nowhere in the developing world do states have the wherewithal to police the use of resources throughout the territory they claim as public domain. In one region of Irian Jaya, Indonesia, for example, just five government foresters monitor

> "Few states recognize indigenous peoples' rights over homelands, and where they do, those rights are often partial, qualified, or of dubious legal status."

110,000 square kilometers of lands. Lacking even motorized vehicles, they have never visited most of the forests they are charged with managing.[39]

Few states recognize indigenous peoples' rights over homelands, and where they do, those rights are often partial, qualified, or of dubious legal status. Countries may recognize customary rights in theory, but enforce common or statutory law against those rights whenever there is a conflict; or they may sanction indigenous rights but refuse to enforce them. Some states reserve lands for indigenous use but refuse indigenous peoples outright ownership; others recognize land rights but retain rights to minerals underground—and even, as in Bolivia, to stands of timber on the land.

Through this cloud of legal contradictions a few countries nonetheless stand out as exceptional. Papua New Guinea, Ecuador, Canada, and Australia acknowledge indigenous titles or rights to extensive areas. (See Table 3.) Still, across all the earth's climatic and ecological zones—from the Arctic tundra to the temperate and tropical forests to the savannahs and deserts—native peoples control slim shares of their ancestral domains. Everywhere, they are in the ironic situation of having to struggle within dominant cultures' legal and political systems, and to couch arguments in terms of Western concepts such as "rights," to defend their traditional control of the resources from which they subsist.[40]

Arctic peoples have won rights to more of their resource base than other indigenous peoples have. In 1971, native communities in Alaska secured rights to 11 percent of the state. In late 1991, negotiations between Canada and the Inuit people resulted in an agreement to create Nunavut, a self-governing region covering one fifth of national territory. Greenland, a self-governing territory of Denmark, is effectively Inuit land because of its overwhelmingly indigenous population, and the Sami have exclusive rights to graze reindeer in about one-third of Sweden. In Russia, however, indigenous peoples of the Arctic lack effective resource rights. There, ethnic autonomous regions created by the Soviet state (encompassing on paper much of Siberia) were powerless against state-sponsored resource exploitation. Prospects appear better in the new Russia, and some reforms are under way.[41]

**Table 3. Areas Legally Controlled by Indigenous Peoples,
Selected Countries, 1992**

Country	Area Legally Controlled[1]	Share of National Territory
	(thousand square kilometers)	(percent)
Papua New Guinea	449	97
Fiji	15	83
Ecuador	190	41
Nicaragua	59	40
Sweden	137	31
Venezuela	234	26
Colombia	260	23
Canada	2,222	22
Panama	15	20
Australia	895	12
Mexico	160	8
Brazil	573	7
New Zealand	16	6
United States	365	4
Costa Rica	2	4

[1]Figures are in most cases liberal. They include area over which, in principle, indigenous peoples have exclusive rights to use land and water bodies. Does not imply recognized indigenous ownership (many states retain ownership of indigenous reserves), or rights to minerals or petroleum (which states often retain). Does not necessarily imply effective state backing and full enforcement of rights. Some indigenous rights to use resources are limited (for example, Sweden recognizes indigenous peoples' rights only to graze reindeer). Figures generally exclude private, individually owned farms of indigenous peoples, as in Andean countries and Mexico.

Source: Worldwatch Institute, based on sources in endnote 40.

In temperate-zone nations, the indigenous land rights situation is mixed. Aboriginal peoples of Japan and Taiwan have no land rights. In contrast, Indian reservations in the United States cover 3 percent of the country (outside of Alaska)—though most of these refuges are infertile drylands. In southern Canada, where Indian reservations are numerous but tiny, crucial legal rulings have denied Indian claims to broader ancient-forest homes since 1990. South of the equator, among the temperate nations of Argentina, Chile, and New Zealand, only the latter has recognized substantial indigenous land— and fishery—rights.[42]

The perhaps 40 million pastoralists who occupy the world's grasslands and drylands have little control over the resources they use along their ancestral nomadic routes. The pastoralists of the Sahel, for example, have extremely few legal guarantees that their seasonal rangelands will remain open to them. In east Africa, the situation is similar, although the Masai have managed to hold on to some of their land base in Kenya and Tanzania by subdividing it into group ranches for registration under national land laws. On the plains of central Asia, pastoralists live in theoretically autonomous regions created for them by China and the former Soviet Union; but only in Mongolia, where herders constitute a majority of the population, have such paper guarantees translated into effective local control over grazing lands.[43]

A few million erstwhile hunter-gatherers also inhabit drylands. Australian aborigines have raised the share of national territory they possess to 12 percent in recent decades. The San of Botswana and neighboring states, in contrast, have no legally reserved land, and only tenuous rights to hunt and forage on fragments of their former home range in the Kalahari Desert. Foraging bands elsewhere in the drylands of Africa are on equally shaky legal footing.[44]

Among the world's tropical forest peoples, South American Indians have substantial land rights (though enforcement has been lacking), Asian peoples have minimal rights even on paper, and African forest dwellers have none. South American nations have been particularly active. In 1989, Colombia recognized Indian rights over much of its Amazon territory. In 1990, Bolivia granted territorial protection to tribes in the jungle region of Beni. In 1991, Venezuela and Brazil reserved lands for the Yanomami—whose home range spans the border of those countries. Together, the two Yanomami reserves are the size of Uruguay. And in 1992, Ecuador set aside much of the Amazon province of Pastaza for Indians. These legal decrees have yet to be translated into effective indigenous control on the ground, and they are marred in most cases by the absence of mineral rights, but they are nonetheless exceptional achievements.[45]

In Asia, tropical forest peoples have fragmentary protection. On the mainland, only the Orang Asli of peninsular Malaysia and the adivasis of India have legal rights over token aboriginal reserves, and those areas are constantly shrinking. The states of Laos, Cambodia, Thailand, and Vietnam—along with China in its neighboring provinces—claim all forestlands, although Laos reportedly plans to map communal forests for tribal villages. The most abusive nations in the region are Bangladesh and, especially, Myanmar. Both are waging war on tribal peoples to deny them control of forested highlands.[46]

In the island nations of Southeast Asia, governments pay lip service to indigenous land rights but disregard them in practice. The Philippine Constitution of 1987 promised swift recognition of indigenous peoples' ancestral domain, for example, but in 1992 the Congress shelved a bill to implement that pledge after five minutes of debate. Indonesia purports to respect *adat*, or customary rights, unless the national interest is at stake; however, the government translates national interest as "economic development," effectively voiding indigenous claims. In the Malaysian province of Sarawak, on the island of Borneo, one-fifth of state land is officially classified as Native Customary Rights Land. Yet just one-tenth of that is actually titled to communities, and even there the government can unilaterally override customary rights for timber concessions.[47]

The most progressive land policies for forest-dwellers in Asia—in force in India and the Philippines—involve joint management agreements between forest services and indigenous communities. Under these "comanagement" or "stewardship" schemes, ownership remains with the state but local people gain recognition of long-term rights to use forest products and make some resource management decisions. Forest agencies are turning to this approach in desperation, realizing that their few thousand employees will never be able to protect or regenerate remote habitats without the help of the millions who live there. (In South America, the government of Bolivia so despaired of patrolling public lands that in 1992 it began to deputize Indians as forest guards.)[48]

In the tropical forests of Africa, even such limited recognition of indigenous peoples' rights is scarce. The pygmies of central Africa, probably the most ancient of all the world's forest peoples, have been left with absolutely no legal rights to their forests in Cameroon and neighboring states. Indigenous homelands, like indigenous peoples, are a forbidden subject in much of Africa, where leaders anxious to avoid fratricidal civil wars in their multiethnic nations have made discussion of customary land claims taboo.[49]

The only bright spots for African forest dwellers are a handful of experimental programs in the dry forests of the southern and eastern parts of the continent. There, embattled conservation agencies overwhelmed by wildlife poachers have turned to local tribes for help in the struggle against game extinctions. Recognizing that indigenous peoples managed elephant and other game long before African states existed, these pilot programs have returned ownership of wildlife to villagers, allowing them to sell quotas of high-priced wildlife products so long as they guard breeding stocks. The results, as in the larger forest stewardship programs in Asia, have been heartening, with ecosystems recuperating and game populations rebounding.[50]

Spreading the joint management approach quickly—and moving beyond it to recognize indigenous land rights—will depend on pressing national governments from all directions. Indigenous movements are doing their part through their grassroots movements, as described later in this paper. The World Bank and the regional development banks, all of which are officially committed to supporting endangered peoples and fostering sustainable development, have yet to take a consistent stand on indigenous rights. Simply conditioning new loans on the demarcation of indigenous lands—or on the institution of joint management—might put thousands of square kilometers of imperiled habitat back into the hands of its rightful stewards.

Even without such gains, however, indigenous peoples deserve widespread recognition for their role as guardians of the natural world. Their cultures occupy a substantial share of the planet's little-disturbed tropical and boreal forests, mountains, grasslands, tundra, and desert, along with large areas of its coasts and near-shore waters. Though they inhabit 12 to 19 percent of the earth's land surface, they have officially sanctioned rights to use, at most, 6 percent. (On paper, native peoples in the Americas—the region for which the best data are available—have exclusive rights to use or have won a degree of autonomous self-govern-ance over 10 percent of land, more than half of it in the Arctic, and are pressing for recognition of rights to 7 percent more.) In effect, indige-nous peoples tend more of the earth than do all park and nature reserve authorities, which together manage 5 percent of the globe's land.[51]

Stewards

Sustainable use of local resources is simple self-preservation for people whose way of life is tied to the fertility and natural abundance of the land. Any community that knows its children and grandchildren will live exactly where it does is more apt to take a long view than a commu-nity without attachments to local places. Moreover, native peoples fre-quently aim to preserve not just a standard of living but a way of life rooted in the uniqueness of a local place. Colombian anthropologist Martin von Hildebrand notes, "The Indians often tell me that the differ-ence between a colonist [a non-Indian settler] and an Indian is that the colonist wants to leave money for his children and that the Indians want to leave forests for their children."[52]

In most native cosmologies, furthermore, nature is more than a store-house of resources. Says Salvador Raín of the Mapuche of Chile, "Our relationship with our god Guinechén is expressed through the land. It is where we develop our culture and bury our dead." Like the Mapuche, many indigenous cultures view nature as inherently valuable, revere it as an embodiment of the divine, or honor it as the home of ancestors' spirits. Their religious beliefs are manifested in the rituals of offering, thanksgiving, and spiritual cleansing so commonly required of those who take fish, game, or trees from their domain. Amid the endless vari-

> **"Any community that knows its children and grandchildren will live exactly where it does is more apt to take a long view than a community without attachments to local places."**

ety of indigenous belief, there is striking unity on the sacredness of ecological systems.[53]

Indigenous peoples' veneration for the natural world has its parallel in their peerless ecological knowledge. Most forest-dwelling tribes are masters of botany. The Shuar people of Ecuador's Amazonian lowlands, for example, use 800 species of plants for medicine, food, animal fodder, fuel, construction, fishing, and hunting supplies. Traditional healers in southeast Asia rely on as many as 6,500 medicinal plants, and shifting cultivators throughout the tropics frequently sow more than 100 crops in their forest farms.[54]

Native peoples commonly know as much about ecological processes that affect the availability of natural resources as they do about those resources' diverse uses. South Pacific islanders can predict to the day and hour the beginning of the annual spawning runs of many fish. Whaling peoples of northern Canada have proved to skeptical western marine biologists that bowhead whales migrate under pack ice. Coastal aborigines in Australia distinguish between 80 different tidal conditions.[55]

Specialists trained in western science often fail to recognize indigenous knowledge because of the cultural and religious forms in which indigenous peoples record and transmit it. Ways of life that developed over scores of generations could only thrive by encoding ecological sustainability into the body of practice, myth, and taboo that passes from parent to child.

The most trivial of customs can have ecological significance. Kayapó women in the Brazilian Amazon, for instance, traditionally grind red ants to make their face paint for maize festivals. North American anthropologist Darrell Posey asked them why and was told, "the little red ant is the friend of the manioc [cassava]." Ecological studies confirmed their explanation. Manioc produces a nectar that attracts ants; the ants, trying to get at the nectar, chew through wandering bean vines that otherwise smother manioc stems. The beans, in turn, are left to climb neighboring corn stalks, where they do no harm. Indeed, corn benefits from the nitrogen that beans add to soil. Red ants thus boost yields of Kayapó women's three staple crops—manioc, beans, and corn.[56]

30 Indigenous peoples use innumerable techniques to husband their forests, grasslands, farms, fisheries, and wildlife. (See Table 4.) On Brazil's Rio Negro, for example, where flood waters regularly inundate low-lying plains and give fish critical but short-lived access to the forest floor, Tukano Indian tradition prohibits farming on the flood plain. The Tukano consider these riparian habitats the property of the fish. Tribal law also sets aside broad areas of the watercourse as fish sanctuaries, where fishing is strictly forbidden; the prohibition is backed up by the belief that the ancestors of the fish will kill one Tukano child for each fish caught in a reserved stretch of the river. Around the world, the techniques of indigenous conservation vary widely, and traditional conservation methods, like modern ones, differ in their effectiveness. But while the means vary, the end—survival over the long term—is universal.[57]

The quality of native stewardship is also evident in comparisons of the ecological condition of indigenous lands with that of neighboring lands managed by others. The island of New Guinea—divided politically between the Indonesian province of Irian Jaya and the independent country of Papua New Guinea—has more distinct cultures than any comparable land area on earth, with more than one sixth of the world's languages on an island the size of Turkey. Of all the world's major tribal areas, New Guinea was the last to be reached by outsiders, who have made contact with inland peoples only within the last 30 years. Most of Papua New Guinea is controlled by leaders of local tribes under customary land rights, while in Irian Jaya, land management decisions are made exclusively by the state. The consequences for local peoples, natural habitats, and social equity are clear: In Papua New Guinea, although indigenous groups have sold resources from their homelands to loggers and miners, they have done so slowly, without devastating their own cultures, and have received some of the profits. In Irian Jaya, indigenous peoples have had their resources stolen, their cultures devastated, and their subsistence economies gutted. Indonesia has designated three-fourths of the province's forests for timber concessionaires.[58]

Ingenious as customary stewardship arrangements are, they are also vulnerable. When pressures come to bear from the cash economy, powerful

**Table 4. Selected Traditional Stewardship Techniques
of Indigenous Peoples**

Resource/ Ecosystem	Stewardship Technique
Forest	Lacondon Maya of southern Mexico plant intricate tree gardens, mimicking the diversity of natural rain forests. Tribal peoples of India revere and protect certain trees as sacred. Gorowa of Tanzania, like the Gabra of Kenya, reserve ancient forest groves as sacred sites dedicated for coming-of-age rituals, men's and women's meeting places, and burials. Karen tribal elders in Thailand carefully regulate community use of forested watersheds.
Grassland	Sukuma, south of Africa's Lake Victoria, rotate grazing on a 30- to 50-year cycle. Zaghawa of Niger move their camels and sheep north to wet-season Saharan pastures in separate, parallel paths, leaving ungrazed strips for the return trek. Fulani orchestrate the orderly return of thousands of head of livestock to the Niger delta in early dry season to avoid overgrazing.
Waters	Temple priests in highlands of Bali distribute irrigation water to farmers through networks of channels, with synchronized rotation ensuring fairness, maximum yields, and minimum pest damage. In mountains of Iran, long-lived gravity-powered quanat system provides irrigation water through elaborate excavations and recharging of groundwater.
Fisheries	In South Pacific, ritual restrictions based on area, season, and species prevent overfishing; religious events often open and close fishing seasons. In Marquesas islands, chieftains forbid the consumption of certain fish and enforce the ban, in extreme cases, by expulsion from island. Wet'suwet'en and Gitksan of Canadian Pacific believe salmon spirits give their bodies to humans for food but punish those who waste fish, catch more than they can use, or disrupt aquatic habitats.

Source: Worldwatch Institute, compiled from sources in endnote 57.

modern technologies, and encroaching populations—or, occasionally, from their own growing numbers—native stewards are likely to find their traditional approaches to management collapsing. The results for nature are catastrophic. In these circumstances, indigenous peoples—like anyone else—are prone to overuse resources, overhunt game, and sell off timber and minerals to pay for consumer goods. Indeed, Alaskan natives have scarred their lands with some of the worst clear-cuts in the United States, and members of the Philippine Manobo tribe now hunt for wild pigs by packing explosives into overripe fruit. Similarly, when new roads in West Kalimantan, Indonesia, made ironwood logging profitable in the late eighties, young men of the Galik tribe bought or borrowed chain saws and rapidly cleared the forest of the ancient trees.[59]

What are the conditions in which traditional systems of ecological management can persist in the modern world? Based on the diverse experience of indigenous peoples, three necessary conditions stand out. First, traditional stewardship's persistence depends on indigenous peoples having secure rights to their subsistence base—rights that are not only recognized but enforced by the state and, ideally, backed by international law. Latin American tribes such as the Shuar of Ecuador, when threatened with losing their land, have cleared their own forests and taken up cattle ranching, because in Latin America these actions prove ownership. Had Ecuador defended the Shuar's land rights, the ranching would have been unnecessary.[60]

Second, indigenous ecological stewardship can survive the onslaught of the outside world if indigenous peoples are organized politically and the states in which they reside allow democratic initiatives. The Khant and Mansi peoples of Siberia, like most indigenous people in the former Soviet Union, were nominally autonomous in their customary territories under Soviet law, but political repression precluded the organized defense of that terrain until the end of the eighties. Since then, the peoples of Siberia have begun organizing themselves to turn paper rights into real local control. In neighboring China, in contrast, indigenous homelands remain nothing more than legal fictions because the state crushes all representative organizations.[61]

Third, if they are to surmount the obstacles of the outside world, indigenous communities need access to information, support, and advice from friendly sources. The tribal people of Papua New Guinea know much about their local environments, for example, but they know little about the impacts of large-scale logging and mining. Foreign and domestic investors have often played on this ignorance, assuring remote groups that no lasting harm would result from leasing parts of their land to resource extractors. If the forest peoples of Papua New Guinea could learn from the experience of threatened peoples elsewhere—through supportive organizations and indigenous peoples' federations—they might be more careful.[62]

A handful of peoples around the world have succeeded in satisfying all three of these conditions. One example is the salmon-based cultures of the Pacific Northwest. In treaty negotiations a century ago, the U.S. government promised these cultures permanent access to their customary fishing grounds both on and off reservations, in exchange for territorial concessions. But starting early in this century, non-Indian fishers began to take most of the catch, leaving little for Indians. The native fishing industry dwindled, and by mid-century had almost died, until the Indians organized themselves to demand their rights. Eventually, in a series of landmark legal rulings in the seventies, U.S. courts interpreted the treaties as reserving half of all disputed fish for Indians.[63]

Their rights secured, the tribes have once again become accomplished fishery managers—rejuvenating their traditional reverence for salmon and training themselves in modern approaches with the help of supportive non-Indians. As stipulated under the court rulings, state and federal fisheries regulators have agreed with qualified tribes to manage fish runs jointly. Today, the Lummi, Tulalip, Muckleshoot, and other Northwestern tribes are managing the salmon runs that nourished their ancestors.[64]

A similar case can be found in Namibia, where most of the San—after a century in which their population declined by 80 percent and their land base shrank by 85 percent—are now day laborers on cash-crop plantations. In the eighties, however, some 48 bands of San, totalling about 2,500 individuals, organized themselves to return to the desert homes they had tenuous rights over. There they have created a modified version of their ancient hunting and gathering economy. With the help of anthropologists, they have added livestock and drip-irrigated gardens to the daily foraging trips of their forebears, fashioning a way of life that is both traditional and modern.[65]

Perhaps because natural resource rights are best recognized in the Americas, indigenous groups there are furthest advanced in adapting traditional resource management arrangements to the modern setting. In northern Canada, the Inuvialuit people have created management plans for grizzly and polar bears and for beluga whales. In southern Mexico, the Chinantec Indians are gradually developing their own blend of timber cutting, furniture making, butterfly farming, and forest preservation in their retreat in the Juarez mountains. The Miskito Indians of Nicaragua's Atlantic Coast, meanwhile, are forming local management groups to police the use of forests, wetlands, and reefs in the extensive Miskito Coast Protected Area they helped create in 1991.[66]

As they struggle to adapt their natural resource stewardship to modern pressures, indigenous peoples are beginning to pool their expertise. The Native Fish and Wildlife Service in Colorado, formed by a coalition of North American tribes, serves as an information clearinghouse on sustainable management. The Kuna of Panama—whose tribal regulations on hunting turtles and game, catching lobsters, and felling trees fill thick volumes—have convened international conferences on forest and fisheries management. The Inuit Circumpolar Conference, representing Inuit peoples from Canada, Greenland, Russia, and the United States, has developed an Inuit Regional Conservation Strategy that includes tight controls on wildlife harvesting and resource extraction, and collaborative arrangements for sharing ecological knowledge. Such instances are still exceptional, but they blaze a trail for indigenous peoples everywhere.[67]

Where the basic conditions of land or water rights, political organization, and access to information are satisfied, two additional and relatively recent developments—new approaches to trade and intellectual property rights—could further assist indigenous communities' efforts to sustain their systems of stewardship against outside forces. These developments also promise native peoples greater control over their interaction with the money economy.

> "Indigenous peoples have painstakingly studied their environments, and their knowledge has aided billions of people elsewhere."

Alternative traders, organizations committed to cultural survival and environmental sustainability, now market millions of dollars worth of indigenous peoples' products in industrial countries. The Mixe Indians of southern Mexico, for example, sell organic coffee to U.S. consumers through the Texas-based alternative trade organization Pueblo to People. The Kayapó sell Brazil-nut oil for use in hair conditioners to the U.K.-based alternative trader The Body Shop.[68]

35

By eliminating links from the merchandising chain, Pueblo to People, The Body Shop, and other alternative traders keep more of the product value flowing back to indigenous producers. The potential for alternative trade to grow is enormous, given the growing purchasing power of environmentally conscious consumers and the abundance of plant products hidden in indigenous lands. Mexico's forests hold an estimated 3,000 useful substances known only to Indians. Among the Quechua of lowland Ecuador, each hectare of forest yields fruits, medicinal plants, and other products worth $1,150 per year in Ecuadorean urban markets. While trade will never make indigenous peoples rich, it can provide them with a modest cash income to supplement their subsistence. Admittedly, harvesting wild products for national and international markets has its risks: it can fuel overexploitation of resources and create schisms within communities. Still, in a world where money is power, no group can survive long without some source of revenue.[69]

A newer route to assuring indigenous peoples a basic income traverses the legal terrain of intellectual property rights—proprietary rights to ideas, designs, or information most commonly typified by patents and copyrights. Indigenous peoples have painstakingly studied their environments, and their knowledge has aided billions of people elsewhere, when, for example, their medicinal plants became the sources of life-saving drugs. Hundreds of years ago the highland Quechua of Peru revealed to Europeans the anti-malarial medicine quinine; the lowland Indians of the Amazon showed them how to make the emetic ipecac; and the peoples of the Guyanas instructed them on extracting from plants the muscle-relaxant curare, which was used in abdominal surgery for a century.[70]

Yet indigenous peoples have rarely received anything of commensurate value in return; indeed, they have sometimes been annihilated for their efforts. One fourth of the coal the Soviet Union dug up during its seven-decade history came from the lands of the Shorish people of Western Siberia. The destruction that mining unleashed after the Shors disclosed the locations of the minerals has whittled them down to a few hundred survivors. In Guyana, likewise, the Macushi tribe revealed the ingredients of their blow-dart poison to English naturalist Charles Waterton in 1812. Scientists used that recipe to develop curare. The tribe—dispossessed, uprooted, and alienated from its culture in the intervening period—now lives in misery, not even remembering how to make blow guns.[71]

The potential payoff for establishing indigenous peoples' rights to their knowledge is enormous, as the case of prescription medicines illustrates. One-fourth of prescription drugs dispensed by U.S. pharmacies are derived from plants. Of those plant-derived active ingredients, approximately three-fourths have similar uses in traditional, herbal medicine, according to pharmacologist Norman R. Farnsworth of the University of Illinois in Chicago. Many were developed by following the lead of indigenous healers. Annual sales of plant-derived drugs in the United States alone total $8 billion, so even if indigenous peoples earned only a fraction of one percent in royalties for their contributions to drug development, the cash flow would be substantial.[72]

With the explosive growth in biotechnology since 1980, the demand for new genetic material is burgeoning. Many of the world's genes are in the millions of species in the endangered places known only to endangered peoples. Indeed, some indigenous leaders think of the rush to codify and exploit indigenous knowledge of biological diversity as the latest in the long history of resource grabs perpetrated against them. "Today," says Adrian Esquina Lisco, spiritual chief of the National Association of Indigenous Peoples of El Salvador, "the white world wants to understand the native cultures and extract those fragments of wisdom which extend its own dominion." Still, supporters of indigenous peoples are developing legal strategies to turn the gene trade to native advantage by demanding recognition that indigenous communities possess intellectual property rights as valid as those of other inventors and discoverers.[73]

> "One-fourth of prescription drugs dispensed by U.S. pharmacies are derived from plants. Of those plant-derived ingredients, three-fourths have similar uses in traditional herbal medicine."

Native peoples' cultural ties to their local environments predispose them to guard and conserve the flora and fauna of their ancestral homes, but they need rights to their subsistence base, a degree of political organization, and support from allied segments of the world beyond their borders to translate that cultural predisposition into sustainable development. The world's indigenous peoples expend much of their energy simply trying to secure the first of those conditions: resource rights. To date, their successes have been few. But there is reason to expect greater success in achieving this first condition as advances continue in the second and third conditions—indigenous political mobilization and support from nonindigenous people.

Rising from the Frontier

From the smallest tribal settlements to the U.N. General Assembly, indigenous peoples organizations are making themselves felt. Their grassroots movements have spread quickly since 1970, strengthening their political skills, recruiting ever more members, and adapting their cultural techniques of self-defense to the political circumstances in which they find themselves. Everywhere, indigenous peoples have concluded that, in the words of Fernando Manling of the Kankanaey people of the northern Philippines, "the only way is to organize."[74] They have pooled their talents in regional, national, and global federations to broaden their influence. This uprising, which like any movement has its share of internal rivalries, may bring fundamental advances in the status of all endangered cultures.

The nature of the organizing process is evident in the case of Mount Apo. There, Chief Tulalang Maway and his people opposed plans to tap the mountain's internal heat for geothermal energy from the time the Philippine National Oil Company proposed it in the mid-eighties. Geothermal energy is renewable and relatively clean, but developing it on Mount Apo requires clearing primary forests high up the mountain, degrading the habitat of endangered species like the Philippine eagle, and intruding on the nation's oldest national park.[75]

In 1989, when their other protests had failed, Maway and 20 other

Lumad elders performed a sacred ritual called D'yandi, committing themselves, their people, and all their Lumad descendants to protecting

Mount Apo with their lives. Explaining the motivation for this firm stance, he quietly recounted the creation myth passed down to him from his great-great-grandfather. In the tale, the creator of the world, Apotio, bids the Lumad farewell and goes to his resting place in Mount Apo after finishing his work: "Apotio told us," said Chief Maway, "'Guard this place, never let anyone destroy or desecrate this place. You may suffer hardships and poverty, but never leave this place because this is where I live.... Never give the mountain. It is better for you to die, to die rather than to give this mountain.'"[76]

The D'yandi—and the nonviolent blockades of the construction site that the Lumad periodically carry out—has drawn others to their cause, including Philippine environmentalists and human rights advocates such as the Legal Rights and Natural Resources Center. That organization, a group of young lawyers who have set themselves the task of overturning Philippine law's utter disregard for indigenous land rights, challenged the project's sketchy environmental impact assessment before the Supreme Court, seeking an injunction to halt construction. Despite a meticulously documented case, the Supreme Court dismissed the motion on a technicality.[77]

While legal arguments swirled, a national Save Mount Apo movement was gaining momentum, finding supporters even within municipal, provincial, and national government. Through the Philippine federation of indigenous peoples, the Lumad reached out overseas, hoping to augment their domestic campaign with foreign pressure. Lumad representatives pleaded their case at international conferences in New York, Seattle, Tokyo, and Santiago, Chile. In a major victory, the Lumad and their allies even convinced the World Bank to deny financing to the project because of its intrusion onto tribal lands.[78]

In 1992, however, five army and marine battalions encamped themselves around the mountain, ostensibly to ward off attacks from communist guerrillas, but mostly to intimidate the Lumad. Death threats against indigenous leaders began to come at regular intervals—including a widely reported $1,600 reward allegedly put on the head of Chief

Maway by unnamed parties associated with the project. The Philippine National Oil Company vehemently denied any involvement in the plot, but a cloud of intimidation and fear nonetheless cloaked the mountain.[79]

Finally, some of the Lumad broke ranks and accepted the terms of the company, which promised that if the plant was completed, it would establish a foundation for supportive Lumad and put more than $250,000 a year into it. Capitalizing on the disarray in the Lumad camp, construction crews high on the flanks of the mountain moved quickly to clear-cut forests and begin drilling wells. In mid-1992, Maway and those loyal to the D'yandi were regrouping for a full-fledged blockade of the construction site. In the quiet before the storm, the chief was steadfast, "I'm old. If they kill me, others will take my place."[80]

As in every place where indigenous peoples stand between industrial developers and ancestral lands, the Lumad confront an adversary better equipped, financed, and connected with centers of power than they are. All that the Lumad have on their side is the strength of their convictions. Their experience is unusual only in the degree of support they have received from afar. The long odds, the struggle to reinterpret traditional institutions such as D'yandi, the intimidation, the threats of violence, the danger of factionalism within the community, and the elusiveness of victory are characteristic of such confrontations worldwide.

Still, victory does sometimes come. In Ecuador, for example, Indians have mounted a dramatic and effective campaign to claim their due. After centuries of second-class citizenship, they want to secure not only rights to the lands they have worked since time immemorial, but also constitutional recognition of their distinct cultures. In June 1990, after decades of grassroots organizing, Ecuador's Indian federations called their people to march peacefully on the cities, to blockade the nation's highways, and to refuse to sell food outside their communities. For three days, a million Indians brought the country to a standstill; enraged as they were, the ruling classes had no choice but to take heed as the Indians enumerated their priorities. High on the list were 72 land claims languishing in the bureaucracy.[81]

Negotiations with the government begun that watershed week in 1990 continued with little progress until a new march began in 1992. This time 2,500 marchers set out from the jungle lowlands of Pastaza province, heading for the mountain capital of Quito. As the marchers gained altitude, they gained support, swelling to 10,000 when they reached the seat of government in April. There, with the weight of national opinion behind them, they won rights to 12,000 square kilometers of their forest homeland.[82]

"The reason why in recent times the indigenous peoples have been having so much success," observes Albino Pereira Cece of the Kinikinau people of Brazil in a statement that applies equally to Ecuador, "is that indigenous peoples from many different places have come together and united to fight a common battle, to stand together." As Ecuador's Huaorani—the least assimilated tribe in the nation—have struggled against oil development on their land in the extreme east of the country, other tribes have come to their aid. The Confederation of Indian Nationalities of the Ecuadorean Amazon, using a technique perfected by the Awa people of Ecuador's extreme west, is helping them clear a boundary strip around their territory and post it against trespassers. The Awa, meanwhile, have aided their tribe members in the contiguous zone of neighboring Colombia to demarcate their land, and have convinced both national governments to recognize the area as an international ethnic forest reserve.[83]

Unity among indigenous peoples is growing steadily as networks spread, linking community groups into tribal federations, tribal federations into national confederations, and national confederations into international unions. For many cultures, long accustomed to antagonistic relations with neighboring peoples, making common cause does not come easily. Indeed, the indigenous movements that now offer hope for the survival of endangered cultures are, ironically, often clothed in the political or legal language of the world's dominant cultures. Nevertheless, the tendrils of these pan-indigenous organizations are seeking each other across mountain ranges and bodies of water, interlocking where they meet, and growing into tough and pliable vines of mutual support and joint resistance. To one degree or another, this process is occurring everywhere—among dryland hunter-gatherers in southern Africa and the Australian outback, grassland pastoralists in the

> **"Indigenous peoples organizations are most abundant and successful where societies are democratic, and where legal channels for the defense of human rights are open."**

Sahel and central Asia, fishers on the Pacific Rim, and forest-dwellers on all continents.

The situation in Central America, as described by anthropologist Mac Chapin of Cultural Survival, is typical: "In Belize, the Garifuna have formed the National Garifuna Council, and the Kekchi and Mopan Maya have set up the Toledo Maya Cultural Council. These organizations are now part of the Caribbean Organization of Indigenous Peoples (COIP), which also includes newly formed groups from Dominica, St. Vincent, and Guyana. The Cabecar and Bribri peoples of Costa Rica are reviving the tradition of councils of elders as a means of building cohesion in their communities and defending their rights in collective fashion. The Kuna of Panama, who enjoy a long tradition of strong political organization, have been serving as advisors to the Embera, the Wounan, and the Guaymi in their attempts to build organizational strength. Even in Honduras and El Salvador, faint murmurings have been heard from the long-dormant indigenous populations."[84]

So universal is the indigenous uprising of recent decades that Chapin's account of Central America could be extended, without changing its tone or basic theme, to every country where native peoples dwell. The only thing that seems capable of preventing indigenous movements from emerging is political repression. Indigenous peoples organizations are most abundant, and most successful, where societies are democratic and where legal channels for the defense of human rights are open—in countries such as Canada, New Zealand, Sweden, and the United States. Democracy is not a sufficient condition for cultural survival, of course. U.S. democracy, for example, has not stopped the government from violating most of the treaties it signed with Indian tribes. Still, without democratic rights to organize and argue their case, indigenous peoples have little prospect of defending themselves.

In undemocratic societies, these movements have more difficulty gaining ground. Cameroon, like most of Africa's autocratic regimes, follows an avowedly assimilationist policy; the only "right" forest-dwellers have there is to integrate into modern society. The tens of millions of indigenous peoples in China, likewise, have few hopes while that country squelches all independent political organizing. With the doors of state closed to them, indigenous peoples under repressive regimes sometimes take up arms, as they have in Myanmar and parts of Indonesia.[85]

At the local level, even indigenous peoples who are not organized into larger movements commonly resist outside encroachment. In Thailand, remote hill tribes have stood up to illegal loggers backed by the military. The Nahuatl of Mexico have evicted oil prospectors from their lands, defeated a proposed hydroelectric dam, and stalled a plan to bisect their territory with a super-highway. In India, tribal communities have defended their lands against state-sponsored tea plantations, loggers, and commercial reed collectors, frequently without the benefit of supportive national networks.[86]

When local groups make common cause with like-minded others, however, their resistance has greater effect. The indigenous peoples of Siberia have banded together into ever larger federations, enabling them to slow the reckless extraction of timber, petroleum, and gems from their lands even as they press for real control of their herding, hunting, and fishing grounds. The Penan of Malaysian Borneo have repeatedly blocked logging roads to save their home range. Organizing efforts at home and abroad have transformed their efforts from a local nuisance into an international *cause célèbre*, and mistreatment of the Penan has tarnished Malaysia's reputation abroad.[87]

As grassroots movements advance they sometimes turn to electoral politics, as in Chile, where the Mapuche people have spearheaded efforts by the nation's 1 million native people to form their own political party, called Land and Identity. The Ainu of Japan ran a candidate—though unsuccessfully—for the national parliament, the Diet, in 1992, and similar electoral initiatives have been mounted everywhere from Botswana to Malaysia. In Sweden and Norway, the Sami have organized parliaments that present unified policy positions to the legislatures.[88]

Elsewhere, indigenous movements set their sights on national constitutions. In Mexico, Indians are calling for an amendment to enshrine land rights, like those achieved by Brazilian Indians in that country's constitutional convention of 1988. Colombian Indians won representation in the nation's constitutional assembly in 1991, and Canadian indigenous

> "As guardians and stewards of fragile ecosystems,
> indigenous cultures could play a crucial role
> in safeguarding humanity's planetary home."

peoples may win recognition of the right to self-government.[89]

Some indigenous movements have also mastered use of communications media. Brazil's Kayapó tribe takes video cameras to meetings with politicians to record the promises they make. Aboriginal groups in Australia publish newspapers reflecting their culture. And 2 million Aymara Indians in Bolivia, Peru, and Chile tune their radios to Radio San Gabriel for Aymara language news, music, and educational programming.[90]

Legal cases play an important part in native movements in places where the rule of law is strong. North American tribes now have a generation of talented lawyers who turn what they call "white man's law" to Indian advantage, winning back ancestral land and water rights. Maori organizations in New Zealand catalyzed the creation of a special tribunal to investigate violations of the century-old Waitangi treaty, which guaranteed Maori land rights. The tribunal is charged with sifting through claims that cover 70 percent of the country and many of its offshore fisheries.[91]

Regional and global meetings on the rights of indigenous peoples are now commonplace. In June 1992, for example, three separate conferences of native peoples were held in Rio de Janeiro, one preceding and two coinciding with the U.N. Conference on Environment and Development.[92]

The longest-lived series of meetings, and perhaps the most important, has been the annual sessions of the Geneva-based U.N. Working Group on Indigenous Populations. Established by the U.N. Human Rights Commission in 1982, the Working Group is drafting a Universal Declaration on the Rights of Indigenous Peoples. The version of late 1992 stated: "Indigenous peoples have the collective and individual right to own, control and use the lands and territories they have traditionally occupied or otherwise used. This includes the right to full recognition of their own laws and customs, land tenure systems and institutions for the management of resources, and the right to effective measures by States to prevent any interference with or encroachment on these rights."[93]

The Declaration follows close on the heels of the International Labor Organization's Convention 169, which took effect in September 1991, calling for respect for the cultural integrity of indigenous peoples. Convention 169 was a considerable improvement upon earlier international documents on native peoples, which encouraged the assimilation and "modernization" of their cultures. The debate has advanced remarkably in recent years, according to attorney Steve Tullberg of the Indian Law Resource Center in Washington, D.C.: "As recently as 1980, any government could stand up in the U.N. and say 'our treatment of our Indians is not your business.' They no longer could." Indeed, the United Nations has declared 1993 International Year of Indigenous Peoples.[94]

The indigenous peoples' cause is also strengthened by a growing movement of advocacy organizations whose members are not native people themselves. These hundreds of organizations may specialize in recording Indian land claims in Brazil, as does the Ecumenical Center for Documentation and Information in São Paulo, or legal aid in the Philippines, as does the Legal Rights and Natural Resources Center in Manila, or any of numerous other tasks. At the international level, organizations such as Cultural Survival, Survival International in London, and the International Work Group for Indigenous Affairs in Copenhagen rally nonindigenous people to the cause. They press recalcitrant governments, spotlight reckless corporations, and prod tradition-bound development funders such as the World Bank to halt their transgressions against endangered cultures.

In a world where almost all nations have publicly committed themselves to the goal of sustainable development and most have signed a global treaty for the protection of biological diversity, the questions of cultural survival and indigenous homelands cannot be avoided much longer. As guardians and stewards of fragile ecosystems and perhaps millions of plant and animal species, indigenous cultures could play a crucial role in safeguarding humanity's planetary home. But they cannot do it alone. They need the support of international law and national policy, and they need the understanding and aid of the world's more numerous peoples.

That understanding has begun to come, in the form of alliances between

Table 5: Priority Actions in Support of Indigenous Peoples

Protect rights of life and liberty.
Indigenous peoples cannot protect their habitats if they lack basic protections against political violence and persecution. International pressure can be applied—for example, in the form of sanctions similar to those used against apartheid South Africa in eighties—against states which conduct or allow acts of genocide, such as those of Guatemala against Mayans, Myanmar against Karen and Shan, and China against Tibetans.

45

Map indigenous homelands.
Definitive maps lend authority and precision to indigenous peoples' territorial claims, and help slow encroachment. Conventional maps need revision. Indonesian government forest maps, for example, show land-use categories of woodlands in detail but do not indicate areas covered by customary rights. Indigenous peoples and supporters could draw new maps, as have indigenous federations in Central America with the aid of Cultural Survival and the National Geographic Society in the United States.

Demarcate and post indigenous domains against trespassers.
Latin American and Philippine tribes are demarcating their lands with boundary clearings and "no trespassing" signs. This serves notice to potential encroachers that indigenous lands are neither empty nor idle.

Create organizations to fight for indigenous rights through the courts.
Many laws to protect indigenous peoples go unenforced. The Toba people of Argentina won assurances in 1924 that their territory would be theirs forever, but they are still waiting for that decree to be put into effect. The Legal Rights and Natural Resources Center in Philippines and Native American Rights Fund in U.S. have achieved some successes by bringing cases to court where there is a chance to prevail under existing law.

Demand strong UN Declaration on Rights of Indigenous Peoples.
The global declaration could become a powerful legal tool and source of moral authority for indigenous peoples. To have full impact, advocates may need to generate popular pressure for a substantive declaration, and actively shepherd it through the U.N. bureaucracy.

Press multilateral development banks to follow tribal peoples policies.
The World Bank and regional development banks have acceptable indigenous peoples policies on paper—including requirements for indigenous land demarcation, social impact assessments, and consultation with indigenous peoples before projects which would affect them can be funded—but violate them frequently in operations.

Source: Worldwatch Institute, compiled from various sources.

indigenous peoples organizations and environmental organizations. For environmentalists, indigenous peoples represent the best hope for preserving the vast, little-degraded habitats encompassed by ancestral homelands. For indigenous peoples, environmentalists are powerful allies, sometimes better skilled in the thrust and parry of modern resource politics. Both sides of this alliance are somewhat wary of the other, divided sometimes by culture, race, and priorities. Still, in the end, indigenous peoples and the environmental movement have much in common. In the words of a young man from the Banwa'on tribe of the Philippines, "Our skins might not be the same color, but our dreams are the same."[95]

The indigenous peoples movement faces a daunting task: defending thousands of distinct cultures and unique local places against the juggernauts of the world economy and population growth. But the experience of indigenous peoples advocates during the eighties points to several strategies as particularly important, because they promise disproportionately large benefits for the energy expended. These include demanding respect for basic human rights to life and liberty; mapping and demarcating indigenous lands; establishing new legal aid groups to exploit already-existing but unenforced pro-indigenous laws in scores of countries; pushing for passage of a strong U.N. Declaration to establish a clear international standard for state actions; and pressing for rigorous implementation of existing indigenous peoples policies at the multilateral development banks—institutions which not only fund the world's largest development schemes but also set the tone and define the terms of development worldwide. (See Table 5.)

Miner's Canary

Half a millenium after Christopher Columbus sailed to the Americas, initiating the geographic expansion of European cultures that has defined modern history, two trends of paramount significance are unfolding that could make the next five hundred years substantially more generous to indigenous peoples than were the last. The end of the Cold War has unfrozen systems of governance, allowing a shifting of political authority from states both downward to local bodies and upward to international ones. It has also allowed the protection of the global environment to rise to a prominent place on the international agenda.

Some of the unfreezing of governance will undoubtedly play itself out in increased nationalism, as it has with tragic effects in the former Yugoslavia in the early nineties. Declarations of national independence have come at a frenzied pace in recent years, to the astonishment of most students of international affairs. Between 1988 and October 1992, the U.N. membership rolls added 16 new names, growing to 178. Such a trend tends to reenforce itself. If Latvians, Czechs, and Eritreans deserve national independence, peoples everywhere are bound to ask themselves, Why not us too? The Oromos of Ethiopia, the Tibetans, the Karen of northern Myanmar, and the Papuans and Timorese of eastern Indonesia have been struggling for autonomy or independence for decades. Scores of other peoples may eventually voice similar demands. Given the underlying cultural divisions that scar Africa and Asia in particular, the number of states could continue to rise swiftly for some time to come. Such a scenario—involving the dissolution of China and various multi-ethnic African states—would have seemed far fetched in the late eighties. In 1992, it is at least conceivable.[96]

In any event, a new assertiveness seems likely: in a world of perhaps 5,000 indigenous cultures, the status of these cultures cannot be ignored. In Canada, for example, when French-speaking Quebec began demanding greater sovereignty in the mid- to late-eighties, Canadian Indians' perennial calls for greater autonomy suddenly gained new prominence. In the United States, tribes on more than a dozen reservations have gained an unprecedented degree of self-rule from the Bureau of Indian Affairs.[97]

The dominance of the nation-state—thought of as seat of all sovereignty—may be near its zenith. The locus of decision-making seems likely to shift downwards to provinces and indigenous domains even as it shifts upwards to regional bodies, such as the European Community, and global bodies such as the United Nations.

Whether or not indigenous peoples win real political autonomy, they stand to benefit from the overarching trends that are transforming governance. On one hand, the decentralization of authority will strengthen their influence over local affairs. On the other hand, its internationalization could give them a means of redress, especially for human rights abuses, higher than the national government. The ultimate result could be a world that values pluralism—a world that celebrates the diversity of cultures and human experiences while respecting as universal the kinds of common values enshrined in the charter of the United Nations and the Universal Declaration on Human Rights. Such principles make clear that, just as indigenous peoples deserve protection from abuse, "culture" does not exonerate them for their own violations of human rights. Violence against women, for example, is tolerated in some indigenous societies—as in the ritual excision of girls' clitorises practiced in parts of Africa, the multiple rapes committed in warfare among the Amazon's Yanomami people, or the female infanticide that continues in some of Asia. A global tapestry of diverse cultures must still have some binding threads.

The rapid degradation of the global environment suggests that one of these universal values should be the objective of passing on to future generations a planet undiminished by the present generation's actions. As this value gains political adherence worldwide, indigenous cultures could benefit. Their qualifications as stewards of ecosystems could increase their prominence and win them long-deserved respect. They may finally be seen as part of the future, as well as of the past.

Indigenous peoples, furthermore, offer the world's dominant culture—a consumerist and individualist culture born in Europe and bred in the United States—living examples of ancient values that may be shared by everyone: devotion to future generations, ethical regard for nature, and commitment to community among people. Such examples are sorely needed, given the impact of the world's materially successful cultures on indigenous peoples' survival. As Anishnabe (Chippewa) leader Winona La Duke said to a North American audience in September 1991, "It is empty to talk . . . so long as this society . . . continues to consume at [this] rate."[98]

Indigenous peoples are also, says Guajiro Indian writer Jose Barreiro, "the 'miner's canary' of the human family." Their cultures, existing in direct and unmediated dependence on the natural realm, are the first to suffer when that realm is poisoned, degraded, or exhausted. Yet in a world threatened by mass species extinction, catastrophic climate change, and industrial contamination of land, air, and water, no culture is safe. In the words of Guarani holyman Pae Antonio, whose Argentine village was burned to the ground in 1991 to make way for a casino: "When the Indians vanish, the rest will follow."[99]

ALAN THEIN DURNING, senior researcher at Worldwatch Institute, investigates the relationships between environmental degradation and social and economic inequality. Mr. Durning is the author of *How Much Is Enough? The Consumer Society and the Future of the Earth* (W.W. Norton & Co., 1992) , co-author of six of the Institute's annual *State of the World* reports, and co-author of Ruth Leger Sivard's *World Military and Social Expenditures 1990–91* (World Priorities, 1991). Among the five previous Worldwatch Papers of which he is author or co-author are *Poverty and the Environment: Reversing the Downward Spiral* (First prize winner in the 1989 World Hunger Media Awards) and *Action at the Grassroots: Fighting Poverty and Environmental Decline*. His articles have appeared in the *Los Angeles Times*, the *Washington Post, Foreign Policy, Technology Review,* and the Institute's bi-monthly magazine *WorldWatch*.

Mr. Durning holds degrees in philosophy and music from Oberlin College and Conservatory. He lives with his wife and son in Takoma Park, Maryland.

Notes

1. Tulalang Maway, Kidapawan, Philippines, private communication, July 9, 1992.

2. *Black Elk Speaks, Being the Life Story of a Holy Man of the Oglala Sioux as Told through John G. Neihardt* (Lincoln: University of Nebraska Press, 1932).

3. Jeffrey A. McNeely, "Common Property Resource Management or Government Ownership," *International Relations*, May 1991.

4. The terms indigenous, native, and tribal are used interchangeably in this chapter for the sake of variety, despite the slight differences in their anthropological meanings. Some indigenous people, as the Hmong of northern Thailand or displaced North American tribes, are not native to their current homes; others—such as the loose bands of pygmies in the Central African rain forest or the millions of Zhuang of China—are not tribal in the anthropological sense. Quechua population from Stefano Varese, "Think Locally, Act Globally," *Report on the Americas*, December 1991, and from Julian Burger, *The Gaia Atlas of First Peoples* (London: Gaia Books Ltd., 1990); Gurumalum of Papua New Guinuea from Barbara F. Grimes, ed., *Ethnologue: Languages of the World*, 11th ed. (Dallas, Tex.: The Summer Institute of Linguistics, Inc., 1988). Table 1 compiled from sources cited throughout this paper. Population figures are Worldwatch Institute estimates, based on close comparison of best available data for each country, from scores of official and independent sources, including those cited as sources for Table 2 in endnote 6. Languages from Grimes, *Ethnologue*.

5. Definition and descriptions of indigenous peoples from Julian Burger, ed., *Indigenous Peoples, A Global Quest for Justice*, a report for the Independent Commission on International Humanitarian Issues (London: Zed Books Ltd., 1987), from Robert Goodland, "Tribal Peoples and Economic Development," World Bank, Washington, D.C., 1982, from Jason W. Clay, "World Bank Policy on Tribal People, Application to Africa," World Bank, Washington, D.C., July 1991, and from Robert K. Hitchcock, "Indigenous Peoples: Working Definitions," in Barbara Johnston, ed., *Human Rights and the Environment* (preliminary draft), Society for Applied Anthropology, Oklahoma City, Okla., May 1992.

6. Language as marker of culture from David Harmon, George Wright Society, Hancock, Mich., "Indicators of the World's Cultural Diversity," presented at Fourth World Congress on National Parks and Protected Areas, Caracas, Venezuela, February 1992. Languages of the world from Michael Krauss, "The World's Languages in Crisis," *Language*, March 1992. Number of indigenous cultures is Worldwatch Institute estimate based on Jason Clay, "Resource Wars: Nation and State Conflicts of the Twentieth Century," in Johnston, *Human Rights and the Environment*, on Burger, *Gaia Atlas of First Peoples*, on Julian Burger, *Report from the Frontier, The State of the World's Indigenous Peoples* (London: Zed Books Ltd., 1987), and on Grimes, *Ethnologue*. Population of indigenous peoples is Worldwatch Institute estimate based on comparison of best available data for each country—from scores of sources—extrapolated to 1992 assuming indigenous populations have kept pace with national population growth, as reported in Population Reference Bureau, *World Population Data Sheet* (Washington, D.C.: various years). Table 2 from Worldwatch Institute estimates based on the following sources: Papua New Guinea, Peru, Chile, Malaysia, Brazil, and former Soviet Union from Burger, *Gaia Atlas of First Peoples*; Bolivia, Ecuador, and Mexico from

Varese, "Think Locally, Act Globally"; Guatemala from Richard N. Adams and Charles Hale, "Sociedad y Etnia: 1930-79," in Edelberto Torres-Rivas, ed., *Historia General de Centroamerica* (Madrid: FLASCO, forthcoming), cited in Anthony R. De Souza, ed., "The Coexistence of Indigenous Peoples and the Natural Environment in Central America," special map supplement to *Research and Exploration* (National Geographic Society, Washington, D.C.), Spring 1992; Myanmar from Martin Smith, independent researcher, London, private communication, June 22, 1992; Laos from Charles F. Keyes, "Tribal Peoples and the Nation-State in Mainland Southeast Asia," in Cultural Survival, *Southeast Asian Tribal Groups and Ethnic Minorities* (Cambridge, Mass.: 1987); New Zealand from 1986 national census cited in Colin James, "Maori Back in the Fold," *Far Eastern Economic Review*, February 15, 1990; Philippines from Ponciano L. Bennagen, Center for Holistic Community, Quezon City, Philippines, private communication, July 15, 1992; India from Moonis Raza and Aijazuddin Ahmad, *An Atlas of Tribal India* (New Delhi: Concept Publishing Company, 1990); Canada from Kimberly Thompson, senior technical officer, Department of Indian and Northern Affairs (INA) Canada, Hull, Quebec, private communication, July 31, 1992; Australia and Thailand from Burger, *Report from the Frontier*; Bangladesh from 1981 official estimate from Minority Rights Group, "Adivasis of Bangladesh," London, December 1991; United States from Evelyn Pickett, public information specialist, U.S. Bureau of Indian Affairs, Washington, D.C., private communication, October 9, 1992.

7. Clay quoted in Elaine Briere and Dan Devaney, "East Timor: The Slaughter of a Tribal Nation," *Canadian Dimension*, October 1990; Brazilian tribes lost from Darcy Ribeiro, *Os Indios e a Civilização* (Rio de Janeiro: Editora Civilização Brasileira, 1970); North American and Australian languages lost from Michael Krauss, professor, Alaska Native Language Center, University of Alaska, Fairbanks, private communication, September 13, 1992.

8. Krauss, "World's Languages in Crisis," and Michael Krauss, Alaska Native Language Center, University of Alaska, Fairbanks, "The Language Extinction Catastrophe Just Ahead: Should Linguists Care?" presented at 15th International Congress of Linguists, Quebec City, Que., Canada, August 10, 1992.

9. Eric R. Wolf, *Europe and the People Without History* (Berkeley: University of California Press, 1982); Alfred W. Crosby, *Ecological Imperialism: The Biological Expansion of Europe, 900-1900* (Cambridge: Cambridge University Press, 1986).

10. William Denevan, ed., *The Native American Population of the Americas in 1492*, 2nd ed. (Madison: University of Wisconsin Press, 1992); population of Europe from Alfred W. Crosby, *The Columbian Exchange, Biological and Cultural Consequences of 1492* (Westport, Conn.: Greenwood Press, 1972); 1992 indigenous population of Americas from Worldwatch Institute estimate based on numerous sources, many but not all of them cited in endnote 6 as sources for Table 2; Australia from J.M. Roberts, *The Pelican History of the World*, rev. ed. (London: Penguin Books Ltd., 1987); New Zealand population contraction from Minority Rights Group, "The Maori of Aotearoa-New Zealand," London, February 1990; Siberia from Demetri B. Shimkin and Edith M. Shimkin, "Population Dynamics in Northeastern Siberia, 1650/1700 to 1970," *Muskox*, Vol. 16, 1975, pp. 6-23.

11. Penan and North American Indians from Burger, *Report from the Frontier*; Sami from

Hugh Beach, "The Saami of Lapland," Minority Rights Group, London, September 1988; Maori from Hitchcock, "Indigenous Peoples: Working Definitions."

52

12. Namibia from Gina Bari Kolata, "!Kung Bushmen Join South African Army," in Robert Gordon, ed., *The San in Transition, Vol. II* (Cambridge, Mass.: Cultural Survival, 1989); Asia Watch, "Bad Blood: Militia Abuses in Mindanao, The Philippines," Human Rights Watch, New York, April 1992; Canadian unemployment from Burger, *Report from the Frontier*, and from Stephen Maly, "Indian Summer," Institute of Current World Affairs (Hanover, N.H.), November 4, 1990; Indian migrant laborers from Brinda Singh, chairperson, Mobile Creches, Delhi, private communication, August 8, 1991; Mexican beggars from José Matos Mar, director, Inter-American Indian Institute, Mexico City, private communication, May 14, 1992; uranium miners from Bill Lambrecht, "Poisoned Lands," *St. Louis Post-Dispatch*, November 19, 1991; Cornelia Ann Kammerer, "Of Labels and Laws: Thailand's Resettlement and Repatriation Policies," *Cultural Survival Quarterly*, Vol. 12, No. 4, 1988; U.S. gambling from Robert W. Venables, "More Than A Game," *Northwest Indian Quarterly*, Fall 1989, and from Edward Walsh, "Rise of Casino Gambling on Indian Land Sparks Controversy," *Washington Post*, June 16, 1992; "Child Prostitution in Taiwan—A National Shame," *Taiwan Church News*, June 1992; adivasis from Alan Whittaker, "Tribal Children: The Superexploited," *Cultural Survival Quarterly*, Vol. 10, No. 4, 1986.

13. Australia from Stephen J. Kunitz, "Public Policy and Mortality Among Indigenous Populations of Northern America and Australasia," *Population and Development Review*, December 1990; Guatemala from Burger, *Report From the Frontier*; India from Raza and Ahmad, *Atlas of Tribal India*; Siberia from Gail Fondahl, professor, Middlebury College, Middlebury, Ver., private communication, October 1, 1992.

14. Thai tribes' lack of citizenship from Kammerer, "Of Labels and Laws: Thailand's Resettlement and Repatriation Policies"; Brazilian Indians legal status from Burger, *Report from the Frontier*.

15. Asia Watch, "Burma: Rape, Forced Labor and Religious Persecution in Northern Arakan," New York, May 7, 1992; Guatemala from Nina M. Serafino, "Latin American Indigenous Peoples and Considerations for U.S. Assistance," Congressional Research Service, Library of Congress, Washington, D.C., August 31, 1991; mass graves from Amnesty International, *Human Rights Violations Against Indigenous Peoples of the Americas* (New York: 1992); East Timor from Ruth Leger Sivard, *World Military and Social Expenditures 1991* (Washington D.C.: World Priorities, 1991); Irian Jaya from Anti-Slavery Society, *West Papua: Plunder in Paradise* (London: 1990); Bernard Nietschmann, professor, University of California, Berkeley, Calif., private communication, October 21, 1992.

16. Quoted in Frederick Kempe, *Siberian Odyssey: A Voyage into the Russian Soul* (New York: G.P. Putnam's Sons, 1992).

17. Gonzalo Aguirre Beltran, *Regiones de Refugio* (Mexico City: Instituto Indigenista Americano, 1967); areas legally controlled and occupied by indigenous peoples are Worldwatch Institute estimates, based on scores of sources, including but not limited to the sources for Table 3 in endnote 40. Area legally controlled is liberal estimate, as detailed in

Table 3.

18. World Council of Indigenous Peoples, "Rights of Indigenous Peoples to the Earth," presented to Working Group on Indigenous Populations, U.N. Commission on Human Rights, Geneva, July 30, 1985; Edtami Mansayagan, secretary general, Alliance of Lumad of Southern Mindanao for Democracy, Kidapawan, Philippines, private communication, July 8, 1992; land rights struggles generally from Roger Plant, "Land Rights for Indigenous and Tribal Peoples in Developing Countries" (draft), World Employment Programme, International Labour Organisation, Geneva, November 1991, from Alan Thein Durning, "Native Americans Stand Their Ground," *World Watch*, November/December 1991, and from Alan Thein Durning, "Last Sanctuary," *World Watch*, November/December 1992.

19. De Souza, "The Coexistence of Indigenous Peoples and the Natural Environment in Central America"; Geodisio Castillo, president, Fundación Dobbo Yala, presentation at American Association for Advancement of Science Annual Meeting, Washington, D.C., February 1991; Philippines from Owen J. Lynch, Jr., and Kirk Talbott, "Legal Responses to the Philippine Deforestation Crisis," *New York University Journal of International Law and Politics*, Spring 1988, and from Therese Desiree Perez, "Philippine Forests: A Case of Disappearance," *Philippine Natural Resources Law Journal*, December 1990; Thailand from Janis B. Alcorn and Owen J. Lynch, "Empowering Local Forest Managers: Toward More Effective Recognition of the Rights, Contributions and Capacities of People Occupying 'Public' Forest Reserves in the Kingdom of Thailand" (draft), Biodiversity Support Program/World Resources Institute, Washington, D.C., August 1992.

20. Figure 1: Highest cultural diversity from Krauss, "World's Languages in Crisis"; megadiversity countries from Jeffrey A. McNeely et al., *Conserving the World's Biological Diversity* (Gland, Switzerland and Washington, D.C.: International Union for Conservation of Nature and Natural Resources et al., 1989).

21. Indonesian rice varieties from *Biodiversity Action Plan for Indonesia* (draft), cited in John C. Ryan, *Life Support: Conserving Biological Diversity* (Washington, D.C.: Worldwatch Institute, 1992); genetic diversity rescuing monocultures from Jack Kloppenburg, Jr., "No Hunting!" *Cultural Survival Quarterly*, Summer 1991.

22. Kpelle farming from Gordon C. Thomasson, "Liberia's Seeds of Knowledge," *Cultural Survival Quarterly*, Summer 1991; International Society for Ethnobiology's 1988 Conference Statement quoted in Panos Institute, "Cultural and Biological Diversity: 'Towards the Edge of the Cliff,'" London, 1992.

23. Arturo Gómez-Pompa and Andrea Kaus, "Taming the Wilderness Myth," *Bioscience*, April 1992.

24. Amazon from William K. Stevens, "Research in 'Virgin' Amazon Uncovers Complex Farming," *New York Times*, April 3, 1990; Central America from Gómez-Pompa and Kaus, "Taming the Wilderness Myth"; animal and plant populations from Jeffrey A. McNeely, "Conserving Cultural Diversity," *Sustainable Development*, Vol. 1, No. 1 (1991).

25. Sami from Hugh Beach, "After the Fallout: Chernobyl and the Sami," *Cultural Survival Quarterly*, Vol. 13, No. 2 (1989); Fishers from Don Hinrichsen, *Our Common Seas* (London: Earthscan, 1990); Nuclear testing from William Le Bon and Bernard Nietschmann, "Nuclear States Bomb Fourth World Nations" (map), *Cultural Survival Quarterly*, Fall 1991.

26. Shelton Davis, "Globalization and Traditional Cultures," *Northeast Indian Quarterly*, Spring 1991.

27. Intrusions on indigenous lands from Burger, *Report from the Frontier*, and from Burger, *A Global Quest for Justice*.

28. Borneo from Wade Davis and Thom Henley, *Penan, Voice for the Borneo Rainforest* (Vancouver: Western Canada Wilderness Committee, 1990); Latin America from Cathy Fogel, associate international representative, Sierra Club, Washington, D.C., private communication, October 12, 1992; Myanmar from Robert Birsel, "Few Winners in Burma's Teak War," *Cultural Survival Quarterly*, Vol. 13, No. 4, 1989, and from Crystal Ashley, human rights consultant to Asia Watch, New York, private communication, June 4, 1992; Marina Roseman, "Temiar Singers of the Landscape: Song, History, and Property Rights in the Malaysian Rainforest," presented at Culture and the Question of Rights in Southeast Asian Environments: Forests, Coasts, and Seas, Woodrow Wilson Center, Washington, D.C., June 3, 1992.

29. American Anthropological Association, "Report of the Special Commission to Investigate the Situation of the Brazilian Yanomami," Washington, D.C., June 1991; demarcation from Vikram Akula, "Drawing the Line," *World Watch*, November/December 1992; mining concessions and Indian lands from Ecumenical Center for Documentation and Information cited in Barbara J. Cummings, *Dam the Rivers, Damn the People* (London: Earthscan Publications Ltd., 1990).

30. Effects of petroleum production generally from Kempe, *Siberian Odyssey*, and from Z.P. Sokolova, "Peoples of the North of the U.S.S.R.: Past, Present, and Future," *Sovetskaya Ethnografiya*, Vol. 6, 1990, as cited by Gail Fondahl, professor, Middlebury College, Middlebury, Vt., private communication, October 1, 1992; lands useless for subsistence from Gail Fondahl, "The Invasion of Siberia," *Cultural Survival Quarterly*, Fall 1992; Cofanes shaman quoted in Nancy Postero and Sandy Tolan, "Oil in Ecuador's Amazon," *Vanishing Homelands: A Chronicle of Change Across the Americas* (radio documentary for National Public Radio, Washington, D.C.), (Tucson, Arizona: Desert West Research and Information, 1992).

31. James Bay projects from Catherine Foster, "Canadian Hydro Project Opposed," *Christian Science Monitor*, March 21, 1991; Coon-Come quoted in Jeffrey Wollock, "James Bay: Down to the Wires," *Native Nations*, January 1991; India from Bradford Morse and Thomas R. Berger, *Sardar Sarovar: Report of the Independent Review* (Ottawa: Resource Futures International Inc., 1992); China from Nicholas D. Kristof, "Dispute Over a Dam on the Scenic Yangtze," *New York Times*, January 21, 1992.

32. Estimated number of small-boat fishers from R. E. Johannes, "Small-Scale Fisheries: A

Storehouse of Knowledge for Managing Coast Marine Resources," presented at Ocean Management Symposium, Smithsonian Institution, Washington, D.C., November 20, 1991; estimated share of fish catch by small-boat fishers from John Cordell, "Introduction: Sea Tenure," in John Cordell, ed., *A Sea of Small Boats* (Cambridge, Mass.: Cultural Survival, 1989); Bernard Nietschmann, "Traditional Sea Territories, Resources and Rights in Torres Strait," in ibid.

33. Charles Lane, "Barabaig Natural Resource Management: Sustainable Land Use Under Threat of Destruction," U.N. Research Institute for Social Development, Geneva, June 1990; Louis A. Picard, *The Politics of Development in Botswana: A Model for Success?* (Boulder, Colo.: Lynne Reinner Publishers, 1987); Australian ranches from Robert Hitchcock, professor, University of Nebraska, Lincoln, private communication, October 2, 1992; Orang Asli from Barbara S. Nowak, "Can the Partnership Last," *Cultural Survival*, Vol. 8, No. 2, 1984.

34. Gloria Davis, "The Indonesian Transmigrants," in Judith Sloan Denslow and Christine Padoch, eds., *People of the Tropical Rain Forest* (Berkeley: University of California Press, 1988); Anti-Slavery Society, *West Papua: Plunder in Paradise*.

35. *Terra nullius* from Olive P. Dickason, "Concepts of Sovereignty at the Time of First Contacts," in *The Law of Nations and the New World* (Edmonton: University of Alberta, 1989), and from William H. Scott, "Demythologizing the Papal Bull 'Inter Caetera,'" *Philippine Studies*, Vol. 35, 1987, pp. 348-56.

36. Gus Gatmaytan, chief of direct legal services, Legal Rights and Natural Resources Center, Quezon City, Philippines, private communication, July 7, 1992; share of Philippines in public domain from Perez, "Philippine Forests: A Case of Disappearance"; Indonesia from Mark Poffenberger, ed., *Keepers of the Forest: Land Management Alternatives in Southeast Asia* (West Hartford, Conn.: Kumarian Press, 1990); Thailand from Alcorn and Lynch, "Empowering Local Forest Managers"; India from Plant, "Land Rights for Indigenous and Tribal Peoples"; Cameroon from Elizabeth A. Halpin, "Indigenous Peoples and the Tropical Forestry Action Plan," World Resources Institute, Washington, D.C., June 1990, and from Kirk Talbott, World Resources Institute, "Nation States and Forest Peoples: Tenurial Control and the Squandering of the Central African Rainforest," presented to Second Annual Meeting of the International Association for the Study of Common Property, Winnipeg, Man., Canada, September 26-29, 1991; Tanzania from Owen J. Lynch, "Whither the People? Demographic and Tenurial Aspects of the Tropical Forestry Action Plan," World Resources Institute, Washington, D.C., September 1990; Australia from Burger, *Report from the Frontier*, and from Ronald T. Libby, *Hawke's Law: The Politics of Mining and Aboriginal Land Rights in Australia* (University Park: Pennsylvania State University Press, 1989).

37. Elinor Ostrom, *Governing the Commons: The Evolution of Institutions for Collective Action* (New York: Cambridge University Press, 1990).

38. Tibet from Jeffrey A. McNeely, "Man and Nature in the Himalaya: What Can Be Done to Ensure that Both Can Prosper?" in Jeffrey A. McNeely et al., eds., *People and Protected Areas in the Hindu-Kush Himalaya* (Kathmandu, Nepal: King Mahendra Trust, 1985).

39. Irian Jaya from Chip Barber, World Resources Institute, Washington, D.C., private communication, September 21, 1992.

56

40. Legal ambiguities from Plant, "Land Rights for Indigenous and Tribal Peoples," and from Ronald Wixman, "Manipulating Territory, Undermining Rights," *Cultural Survival Quarterly*, Winter 1992. Table 3 assembled from scores of sources, including: Papua New Guinea from Owen J. Lynch, "Towards Conservation Partnerships in Papua New Guinea" (draft), World Resources Institute, Washington, D.C. , July 1992; Fiji from Brij Lal, "Politics and Society in Post-Coup Fiji," *Cultural Survival Quarterly*, Vol. 15, No. 2, 1991; Ecuador from Plant, "Land Rights for Indigenous and Tribal Peoples," and from Douglas Farah, "Ecuador Cedes Amazon Lands to Indians," *Washington Post*, May, 4, 1992; Sweden from Beach, "Saami of Lapland"; Colombia from Peter Bunyard, *The Colombian Amazon: Policies for the Protection of its Indigenous Peoples and Their Environment* (Cornwall, U.K.: Ecological Press, 1989); Canada from INA Canada, *Schedule of Indian Bands, Reserves, and Settlements* (Hull, Quebec: 1990), from INA, "Information Sheet No. 9," Ottawa, February 1992, and from INA, "Comprehensive Land Claims in Canada," Ottawa, December 1991; Australia from Libby, *Hawke's Law*, and from Burger, *Report from the Frontier*; Panama from Mac Chapin, program director of resource management, Cultural Survival, Arlington, Va., private communication, June 22, 1992; Mexico from Stefano Varese, professor, University of California, Davis, private communication, September 22, 1992; Brazil from Carlos Alberta Ricardo, Ecumenical Center for Documentation and Information, São Paulo, Brazil, private communication, February 25, 1992; New Zealand from *Asiaweek*, December 23-30, 1988; Nicaragua from Bernard Nietschmann, professor, University of California, Berkeley, private communication, September 15, 1992; United States from Pickett, private communication; Costa Rica from Marcos Guevara Berger and Rubén Chacón Castro, "Territorios Indios en Costa Rica: Origenes, Situacion y Perspectivas," unpublished, January 1992; Venezuela from John Frechione, "The Yekuana of Southern Venezuela," *Cultural Survival Quarterly*, Vol. 8, No. 4, 1984, from Nelly Arvelo-Jimenez and Andrew L. Cousins, "False Promises," *Cultural Survival Quarterly*, Winter 1992, and from APPEN Features, "Venezuela: Yanomami Indians Demand Their Land," Asia-Pacific People's Environment Network, Penang, Malaysia, 1990; India from Council for Advancement of People's Action and Rural Technology, "People's Action," July 1990.

41. Thomas R. Berger, *Village Journey: The Report of the Alaska Native Review Commission* (New York: Hill and Wang, 1985); Government of Canada, "Nunavut Political Accord Initialled," news release, Ottawa, April 27, 1992; Greenland from Burger, *Report from the Frontier*; Sweden from Beach, "Saami of Lapland"; Russia from "After the Breakup," *Cultural Survival Quarterly*, Winter 1992, from International Workgroup for Indigenous Affairs, *Indigenous Peoples of the Soviet North* (Copenhagen: 1990), and from Fondahl, private communication.

42. "Taiwan Church News," June 1992; *Japan Environment Monitor*, May 30, 1991; United States from Pickett, private communication; Canadian reservations from INA Canada, *Schedule of Indian Bands, Reserves and Settlements*; Canadian Indian legal setbacks from Maly, "Indian Summer," from *Cultural Survival Quarterly*, Vol. 15, No. 2, 1991, and from William Claiborne, "The Fight Over Ontario Pine Forest," *Washington Post*, April 22, 1990; German Pollitzer, honorary president, Fundacion Cruzado Patagonica, Buenos Aires, Argentina, private communication, July 16, 1992; Chile from Burger, *Report from the Frontier*; New Zealand from W.H. Oliver, *Claims to the Waitangi Tribunal* (Wellington: Department of Justice, Waitangi Tribunal Division, 1991).

43. Pastoralists' population from S. Sandford, *Management of Pastoral Development in the Third World* (Chichester: John Wiley, 1983); Pastoralists' land rights in general from Paul A. Olson, ed., *The Struggle for the Land* (Lincoln: University of Nebraska Press, 1990); Sahel from H.N. Le Houerou, *The Grazing Land Ecosystems of the African Sahel* (Berlin: Springer Verlag, 1989); Masai from Lee M. Talbot, "Demographic Factors in Resource Depletion and Environmental Degradation in East African Rangeland," *Population and Development Review*, September 1986, and from Solomon Bekure and Ishmael Ole Pasha, "The Response of the Kenya Maasai to Changing Land Policies," in Olson, *The Struggle for the Land*; Russia from Anatoly Khazanov, "Pastoral Nomads in the Past, Present, and Future: A Comparative View," in ibid.; China from Thomas Heberer, *China and Its National Minorities: Autonomy or Assimilation* (New York: M.E. Sharp Inc., 1989); Mongolia from J. Swift and R. Mearns, *The Mongolian Pastoral Economy: Report of an International Workshop* (Rome: FAO, 1991).

44. Australia from Libby, *Hawke's Law*; San from Hitchcock, private communication, October 2, 1992.

45. Land rights in Americas from Durning, "Native Americans Stand Their Ground"; lax enforcement from internal World Bank reports; Bunyard, *Colombian Amazon*; Ramiro López, "Bolivia: Indigenous Win a Battle Over Land," *Latinamerica Press*, September 27, 1990; James Jones, "The March for Dignity: Rationale and Responses for a Native Movement in Eastern Bolivia," *Hunger Notes*, Spring 1991; Venezuela from Arvelo-Jiminez and Cousins, "False Promises"; Brazil from Akula, "Drawing the Line"; Farah, "Ecuador Cedes Amazon Land To Indians."

46. Orang Asli from Nowak, "Can the Partnership Last?"; adivasis from Christoph von Furer-Haimendorf, *Tribes of India: The Struggle for Survival* (Berkeley: University of California Press, 1982), and from Council for Advancement of People's Action and Rural Technology, "People's Action"; Kirk Talbott, "Trip Report: Vientiane, Laos, and Hanoi, Vietnam," World Resources Institute, Washington, D.C., December 1991; "Cambodia," *Cultural Survival Quarterly*, Vol. 14, No. 3, 1990; Thailand from Alcorn and Lynch, "Empowering Local Forest Managers"; Heberer, *China and Its National Minorities*; Minority Rights Group, "Adivasis of Bangladesh"; Martin Smith, *Burma: Insurgency and the Politics of Ethnicity* (London: Zed Books, 1991).

47. Ponciano L. Bennagen, "Tribal Filipinos," in Shelton H. Davis, ed., *Indigenous Views of Land and the Environment* (Washington, D.C.: World Bank, 1991); Ed Legaspi, deputy secretary general, Alliance of Indigenous Peoples Rights Advocates, Quezon City, Philippines, private communication, July 3, 1992; Indonesia from Nancy Peluso, University of California, Berkeley, "Forest Policy—Forest Politics: The Criminalization of Customary Kalimantan," presented at Culture and the Question of Rights in Southeast Asian Environments: Forests, Coasts, and Seas, Woodrow Wilson Center, Washington, D.C., June 3, 1992, and from Sandra Moniaga, WALHI, Jakarta, "Towards Community-Based Forestry

58

and Recognition of Adat Property Rights in the Outer Islands of Indonesia: A Legal and Policy Analysis," presented at Workshop on Legal Issues in Social Forestry, Bali, November 4-6, 1991; Sahabat Alam Malaysia, "Native Customary Rights in Sarawak," *Cultural Survival Quarterly*, Vol. 10, No. 2, 1987; Evelyne Hong, *Natives of Sarawak: Survival in Borneo's Vanishing Forest* (Penang, Malaysia: Institut Masyarakat, 1987).

48. India from Mark Poffenberger, ed., "Forest Management Partnerships: Regenerating India's Forests," Ford Foundation, New Delhi, September 1990; Philippines from Poffenberger, *Keepers of the Forest*; Bolivian Indians example from Shelton Davis, anthropologist, World Bank, Washington, D.C., private communication, April 22, 1992.

49. Cameroon from Talbott, "Nation States and Forest Peoples."

50. Jonathan S. Adams and Thomas O. McShane, *Myth of Wild Africa: Conservation Without Illusion* (New York: W.W. Norton & Co., 1992).

51. Indigenous peoples' total world territory is Worldwatch Institute estimate as described in endnote 17; Indian lands in Americas is Worldwatch Institute estimate based on numerous sources including but not limited to sources for Table 3 in endnote 40; global extent of national parks, nature preserves, and protected areas of similar stature from International Union for Conservation of Nature and Natural Resources, *1990 United Nations List of National Parks and Protected Areas* (Gland, Switzerland, and Cambridge, U.K.: 1990), and from FAO, *Production Yearbook 1989* (Rome: 1990).

52. Hildebrand quoted in James Brooke, "Tribes Get Right to 50% of Colombian Amazon," *New York Times*, February 4, 1990.

53. Raín quoted in *Latinamerica Press*, May 2, 1992.

54. Indigenous ecological knowledge generally from D.M. Warren, ed., "Indigenous Agricultural Knowledge Systems and Development," *Agriculture and Human Values*, Winter/Spring 1991, and from D. A. Posey and W. Balee, eds., "Resource Management in Amazonia: Indigenous and Folk Strategies," *Advances in Economic Botany* (New York Botanical Garden), Vol. 7, 1989; Shuar from Brad Bennett, "Plants and People of Ecuador's Amazonian Rainforests: Lessons and Needs for Sustainable Development," presented at Can Nuts Save the Rain Forest? Symposium, Smithsonian Institution, Washington, D.C., March 25, 1992; Asian healers from Jack Kloppenburg, Jr., "No Hunting!"; shifting cultivators from McNeely, "Conserving Cultural Diversity."

55. South Pacific from Johannes, "Small-Scale Fisheries"; Canadian whalers from Peter Poole, resource management consultant, Alcove, Que., Canada, private communication, May 14, 1992; Australia from Nietschmann, "Traditional Sea Territories, Resources and Rights in Torres Strait."

56. Darrell A. Posey, "Indigenous Ecological Knowledge and Development of the Amazon," in E. Moran, ed., *The Dilemma of Amazonian Development* (Boulder, Colo.: Westview Press, 1983).

57. Tukano from Janet M. Chernela, "Managing Rivers of Hunger: The Tukano of Brazil," *Advances in Economic Botany* (New York Botanical Garden), Vol. 7, 1989. Table 4 sources: Lacandon tree gardens from James D. Nations, "The Lacandon Maya," in Denslow and Padoch, *People of the Tropical Rain Forest*; Indian tribal tree protection from Burger, *Gaia Atlas of First Peoples*; Gorowa sacred groves from C.A. Gerden and S. Mtallo, "Traditional Forest Reserves in Babati District, Tanzania," Swedish University of Agricultural Sciences, International Rural Development Center, Uppsala, 1990; Gabra sacred groves from Maryam Niamir, "Traditional Woodland Management Techniques of African Pastoralists," *Unasylva*, No. 1, 1990; Karen watershed protection from Alcorn and Lynch, "Empowering Local Forest Managers"; all grasslands examples from Niamir, "Traditional Woodland Management Techniques of African Pastoralists"; Bali water temples from Jim Kremer, professor, University of Southern Calif., private communication, November 11, 1992; Iranian quanat from Ian R. Manners, "The Middle East," in Gary A. Klee, ed., *World Systems of Traditional Resource Management* (New York: V.H. Winston & Sons, 1980); South Pacific, including Marquesas, from Gary A. Klee, "Oceania," in ibid; Gitksan and Wet'suwet'en from Mike Morrell, "The Struggle to Integrate Traditional Indian Systems and State Management in the Salmon Fisheries of the Skeena River, British Columbia," in Evelyn Pinkerton, ed., *Co-operative Management of Local Fisheries* (Vancouver: University of British Colombia Press, 1989).

58. Owen J. Lynch, attorney, World Resources Institute, Washington, D.C., private communication, September 21, 1992; Irian Jaya concessions from Anti-Slavery Society, *West Papua: Plunder in Paradise*.

59. Alaska from Michael Wright, senior fellow, World Wildlife Fund, Washington, D.C., private communication, April 20, 1992; Philippines from Linka Ansulang, Carmen, Philippines, private communication, July 9, 1992; Indonesia from Nancy Peluso, "The Criminalization of Customary Kalimantan"; general critique of indigenous resource management from Raymond Hames, "Wildlife Conservation in Tribal Societies," in Margery L. Oldfield and Janis B. Alcorn, *Biodiversity: Culture, Conservation, and Ecodevelopment* (Boulder, Colo.: Westview Press, 1992).

60. Shuar from Chuck Kleymeier, country representative, Inter-American Foundation, Rosslyn, Va., private communication, May 22, 1992.

61. Fondahl, private communication.

62. Lynch, private communication.

63. Pinkerton, *Co-operative Management of Local Fisheries*.

64. Ibid.

65. Robert K. Hitchcock, "Human Rights, Local Institutions, and Sustainable Development Among Kalahari San," presented at 90th Annual Meeting of the American Anthropological Association, Chicago, Ill., November 20-24, 1991; Robert K. Hitchcock, professor, University of Nebraska, Lincoln, private communication, October 1, 1992.

66. Inuvialuit from Dene Cultural Institute, "Amerindian Initiatives in Environmental Protection and Natural Resource Management: A Directory of Projects and Programs" (draft), Yellowknife, N.W. Ter., Canada, 1992; Chinantecs from David Barton Bray, "The Struggle for the Forest," *Grassroots Development*, Vol. 15, No. 3, 1991; Miskitos from Armstrong Wiggins, attorney, Indian Law Resource Center, Washington, D.C., private communication, May 5, 1992.

67. Native Fish and Wildlife Service from Dene Cultural Institute, "Amerindian Initiatives"; Kuna from Chapin, private communication; Inuit conservation strategy from Elaine Smith, ed., *Sustainable Development through Northern Conservation Strategies* (Calgary, Alberta: University of Calgary Press, 1990).

68. Mixe from David Bray, country representative, Inter-American Foundation, Rosslyn, Va., private communication, October 9, 1992; The Body Shop from Julia Preston, "Trial Spurs Debate on Brazil's Indians," *Washington Post*, August 17, 1992.

69. Mexico from Victor Toledo, "Green Economics and Indigenous Wisdom: How Many Products are Enclosed in a Tropical Forest?" presented at Can Nuts Save the Rain Forest? Symposium, Smithsonian Institution, Washington, D.C., March 26, 1992; Ecuador from Bennett, "Plants and People of Ecuador's Amazonian Rainforests," see also Catherine Dold, "Tropical Forests Found More Valuable for Medicine Than Other Uses," *New York Times*, April 28, 1992; risks of alternative trade from John C. Ryan, "Goods from the Woods," *World Watch*, July/August 1991.

70. Intellectual property rights from "Intellectual Property Rights: The Politics of Ownership," *Cultural Survival Quarterly*, Summer 1991; Jack Weatherford, *Indian Givers: How the Indians of the Americas Transformed the World* (New York: Fawcentine Columbine, 1988).

71. Shors from Kempe, *Siberian Odyssey*; Macushi from Mark J. Plotkin, Conservation International, Washington, D.C., untitled presentation at Can Nuts Save the Rain Forest? Symposium, Smithsonian Institution, Washington, D.C., March 25, 1992, and from Mark J. Plotkin, "Strychnos Medeola: A New Arrow Poison from Suriname," in Darrell A. Posey, ed., *Ethnobiology: Implications and Applications, Proceedings of the First International Congress of Ethnobiology* (Belém, Brazil: 1990).

72. Norman R. Farnsworth, "Screening Plants for New Medicines," in E.O. Wilson, ed., *Biodiversity* (Washington, D.C.: National Academy Press, 1988).

73. Adrian Esquina Lisco, "The Pain of Mother Earth," *New Internationalist*, December 1991.

74. Fernando Manling, Dalicno, Philippines, private communication, July 13, 1992.

75. Durning, "Last Sanctuary."

76. Maway, private communication.

77. Gatmaytan, private communication.

78. Mansayagan, private communication; Gatmaytan, private communication.

79. Situation at Mount Apo from Mansayagan, private communication, and from Gatmaytan, private communication; death threat and denial from Carol O. Arguillas, "PNOC Denies Offering Bounty for Tribe Chief," *Philippine Daily Inquirer*, July 13, 1992.

80. Foundation from Victor Mallet, "Getting into Hot Water," *Financial Times*, July 15, 1992; Maway, private communication.

81. Serafino, "Latin American Indigenous Peoples and Considerations for U.S. Assistance."

82. "March on Quito," *South and Meso American Indian Information Center Newsletter* (Oakland, Calif.), Spring/Summer 1992; area recognized from Farah, "Ecuador Cedes Amazon Lands to Indians."

83. Pereira Cece quoted in Karen K. Gaul and R. Brooke Thomas, "Indigenous Perspectives: Ecology, Economy, and Ethics," *Journal of Human Ecology*, special issue No. 1, (1991); Aid for Huaorani from Nina Orville, "Road Construction Threatens Huaorani in Ecuador," *Cultural Survival Quarterly*, Vol. 12, No. 3, 1988; Awa from Theodore Macdonald and Janet Chernela, "Politics, Development, and Indians" (draft), Cultural Survival, Cambridge, Mass., 1992.

84. Chapin, "Contemporary Indians and the Quincentenary."

85. Cameroon from Halpin, "Indigenous Peoples and the Tropical Forestry Action Plan."

86. Thailand from Alcorn and Lynch, "Empowering Local Forest Managers"; Mexico from Curtis Berkey, Steve Tullberg, and Armstrong Wiggins, attorneys, Indian Law Resource Center, Washington, D.C., private communication, May 5, 1992; India from Robert S. Anderson and Walter Huber, *The Hour of the Fox: Tropical Forests, the World Bank, and Indigenous People in Central India* (Seattle: University of Washington Press, 1988).

87. Siberia from Fondahl, private communication; Malaysia from Stan Sesser, "Logging the Rain Forest," *New Yorker*, May 27, 1991.

88. Chile from Alaka Wali, "Living *with* the Land: Ethnicity and Development in Chile," *Grassroots Development*, Vol. 14, No. 2, 1990; Ainu from Reiko Tanaka, "Minorities Seek Gains from Election," *Japan Times*, July 14, 1992; Botswana from Hitchcock, private communication, October 2, 1992; Malaysia from "A Prince is Crushed," *Economist*, October 27, 1990; Sami from International Work Group for Indigenous Affairs, *Self Determination and Indigenous Peoples* (Copenhagen: 1987).

89. Mexico from Robert R. Alvarez, Jr., "The Paipai of Jamau: A Test Case for Constitutional Reform," *Cultural Survival Quarterly*, Vol. 14, No. 4, 1990; Brazil from Linda Rabben, Rain Forest Foundation, Washington, D.C., private communication, April 9, 1992; Colombia from Ted Macdonald, projects director, Cultural Survival, Cambridge, Mass., private communication, March 6, 1992; Canada from Mark Clayton, "Canada's Natives Exercise New Clout on National Scene," *Christian Science Monitor,* July 3, 1992.

90. Kayapó from James Brooke, "Rain Forest Indians Hold Off Threat of Change," *New York Times,* December 3, 1990; Australia from Ron Scherer, "Land Rights News Promotes Cause of Aboriginal People," *Christian Science Monitor,* March 11, 1992; radio from Vicki Elkin, "Radio Wave," *World Watch,* September/October 1992.

91. North American lawyers from José Barreiro, American Indian Program, Cornell University, Ithaca, N.Y., private communication, August 28, 1991; New Zealand from "Old Dreams, New Challenges," *Asiaweek,* December 23-30, 1988.

92. Earth Summit from Rabben, private communication.

93. Draft declaration text from Julian Burger, U.N. Working Group on Indigenous Populations, Geneva, Switerland, private communication, October 8, 1992.

94. Steve Tullberg, attorney, Indian Law Resource Center, Washington, D.C., private communication, May 5, 1992.

95. Anonymous, San Luis Agusan, Philippines, private communication, July 4, 1992.

96. U.N. member countries from United Nations, Department of Public Information, "United Nations Member States," New York, July 31, 1992.

97. Timothy Egan, "Sovereign Once Again, Indian Tribes Experiment with Self-Government," *New York Times,* January 16, 1991.

98. La Duke quoted in Gaul and Thomas, "Indigenous Perspectives: Ecology, Economy, and Ethics."

99. José Barreiro, "Indigenous Peoples are the 'Miner's Canary' of the Human Family," in Bill Willers, ed., *Learning to Listen to the Land* (Washington, D.C.: Island Press, 1991); Cecilia Vaisman and Alan Weisman, "Guarani Indians of Argentina," *Vanishing Homelands.*

THE WORLDWATCH PAPER SERIES

_____ 93. **Water for Agriculture: Facing the Limits** by Sandra Postel.
_____ 94. **Clearing the Air: A Global Agenda** by Hilary F. French.
_____ 95. **Apartheid's Environmental Toll** by Alan B. Durning.
_____ 96. **Swords Into Plowshares: Converting to a Peace Economy** by Michael Renner.
_____ 97. **The Global Politics of Abortion** by Jodi L. Jacobson.
_____ 98. **Alternatives to the Automobile: Transport for Livable Cities** by Marcia D. Lowe.
_____ 99. **Green Revolutions: Environmental Reconstruction in Eastern Europe and the Soviet Union** by Hilary F. French.
_____100. **Beyond the Petroleum Age: Designing a Solar Economy** by Christopher Flavin and Nicholas Lenssen.
_____101. **Discarding the Throwaway Society** by John E. Young.
_____102. **Women's Reproductive Health: The Silent Emergency** by Jodi L. Jacobson.
_____103. **Taking Stock: Animal Farming and the Environment** by Alan B. Durning and Holly B. Brough.
_____104. **Jobs in a Sustainable Economy** by Michael Renner.
_____105. **Shaping Cities: The Environmental and Human Dimensions** by Marcia D. Lowe.
_____106. **Nuclear Waste: The Problem That Won't Go Away** by Nicholas Lenssen.
_____107. **After the Earth Summit: The Future of Environmental Governance** by Hilary F. French.
_____108. **Life Support: Conserving Biological Diversity** by John C. Ryan.
_____109. **Mining the Earth** by John E. Young.
_____110. **Gender Bias: Roadblock to Sustainable Development** by Jodi L. Jacobson.
_____111. **Empowering Development: The New Energy Equation** by Nicholas Lenssen.
_____112. **Guardians of the Land: Indigenous Peoples and the Health of the Earth** by Alan Thein Durning.

_____ **Total Copies**

☐ **Single Copy: $5.00**
☐ **Bulk Copies (any combination of titles)**
   ☐ 2–5: $4.00 each   ☐ 6–20: $3.00 each   ☐ 21 or more: $2.00 each

☐ **Membership in the Worldwatch Library: $25.00 (international airmail $40.00)**
The paperback edition of our 250-page "annual physical of the planet," *State of the World 1993,* plus all Worldwatch Papers released during the calendar year.

☐ **Subscription to *World Watch* Magazine: $15.00 (international airmail $30.00)**
Stay abreast of global environmental trends and issues with our award-winning, eminently readable bimonthly magazine.

No postage required on prepaid orders. Minimum $3 postage and handling charge on unpaid orders.

Make check payable to Worldwatch Institute
1776 Massachusetts Avenue, N.W., Washington, D.C. 20036-1904 USA

Enclosed is my check for U.S. $_____

_____
name   **daytime phone #**

_____
address

_____
city   **state**   **zip/country**